IN THE
SHADOW
OF PACKER

IN THE
SHADOW
OF PACKER

England's Winter Tour of
Pakistan and New Zealand
1977/78

BY DAVID BATTERSBY

First published by Pitch Publishing, 2016

Pitch Publishing
A2 Yeoman Gate
Yeoman Way
Worthing
Sussex
BN13 3QZ
www.pitchpublishing.co.uk

A CIP catalogue record is available for this book
from the British Library.

ISBN 978-1-78531-136-9

Typesetting and origination by Pitch Publishing
Printed by Bell & Bain, Glasgow, Scotland

Contents

For my late father, Alan

Acknowledgements

HOW we take up certain hobbies, whether it is watching, playing or collecting, is arguably hereditary. With me, falling in love with our great game of cricket was down to my father, Alan. It was whilst we were living in Tenby, in West Wales, that I began to watch my dad play for Pembroke Cricket Club, in the Pembrokeshire Cricket League, in the early 1970s. It was my father who was instrumental in buying me my first bat, my first *Playfair Cricket Annual* in 1971 and my first Subbuteo Cricket set not long after. I have great memories of growing up in Pembrokeshire playing cricket with my brother and father, not only on the beach, but also in the garden of our house in Tenby, a house that my dad had proudly built. Playing outside in the summer would be interspersed with dashing inside to catch the latest state of play, in a Test match, or a Sunday John Player League game.

I was born in the early sixties, just north of Newport, and it wasn't until late 1974, when we moved back east, that I was taken regularly by my father to matches at Sophia Gardens in Cardiff to watch Glamorgan and also to the odd game at Worcester or Bristol. It was at these games that I was able to witness, close up, many of the players that featured on England's 1977/78 winter tour.

My father had a strong cricketing heritage. His grandfather, father and uncle all played the game. In fact, his Uncle Dan played many a season for Radcliffe Cricket Club with Sir Frank

Worrell, and also played for the East Lancashire Paper Mills Club, where my great grandfather was involved, along with the South African Test player C.B. Llewellyn.

My father continued to accompany me to matches on and off throughout the many years that followed, until dementia took hold of him. Sadly, he passed away in February 2014. This, my first cricket book, is dedicated to him.

The book has taken several years to write and during that time I would like to thank England players Bob Taylor, Mike Brearley and Bob Willis, who kindly answered questionnaires in the formative stages of writing it. I was most grateful to Bob Willis who provided the foreword to the book, during a very busy time for him working on Sky Television.

Mark Burgess, the New Zealand captain in 1978, was extremely helpful. Mark, kindly and patiently, exchanged several e-mails with me which form the interview in the Appendix section of the book. I was also lucky enough to interview Pakistan opener Mudassar Nazar about his career and scoring the slowest Test century ever recorded, and I thank him for his time in answering all of my questions. A thank you also goes out to all the players I have chatted to over the years at various cricketing outposts about the tour.

I would like to thank Jamie Bell from the New Zealand Cricket Museum, at the Basin Reserve in Wellington, and to Jo Young from the New Zealand Cricket Players Association, who kindly passed on my initial request to Mark Burgess. Jamie was kind enough to point me in the direction of photographer John Selkirk, and several of his photographs appear in the book plate section. Kazz (Karamdeep) Sahota, at Archives New Zealand in Wellington, was most helpful in locating photographs from the tour, some of which appear in the book. My good friend, Mike Ward, gave good advice about the photographs. I would also like to thank John Ward for letting me use part of his interview with Geoff Cope that originally appeared on the Cricket Archive website.

Although my book *In The Shadow of Packer* focuses on events well away from what was happening at the time in Kerry

Packer's World Series Cricket, I thoroughly recommend you read Gideon Haigh's excellent book *The Cricket War – 'The Inside Story of Kerry Packer's World Series Cricket'*.

I must thank Jane and Paul Camillin at Pitch Publishing for all their help and advice in the writing of this book; Graham Hales, for typesetting, and also Duncan Olner for the cover design.

I am indebted to Vic Godding for reading and commenting constructively on my manuscript, as it neared completion. This immense task coincided with a very busy period for him and I am truly grateful for his commitment.

Lastly, but not least, thanks to my wife Donna and my daughter Francesca, for their patience and understanding of my 'obsession' with cricket. Donna has been very supportive of my project and was kind enough to proofread the first draft of the book. Francesca, meanwhile, over the years, has been very good at not complaining about the games she has been dragged along to. But then again, I guess the copious amounts of ice-cream she has been supplied with over the years, as well as in her earlier days of meeting mascots, and having her face painted, might have had something to do with it!

Foreword by Bob Willis

1977 and the game of cricket is in turmoil. Kerry Packer has recruited most of the best players on the planet for his World Series enterprise. The losing Australian tourists to England were split down the middle and presented a disunited front on the field. England announced a mixture of experience and youth in their touring party to Pakistan and New Zealand.

We were to spend ten long weeks in the sub-continent before six far more enjoyable ones down under. The cricket in the first part of the tour produced some of the most boring ever played on the field, but off it some of the most controversial episodes ever.

New Zealand won their first Test against England in the second part of the trip. Brearley broke his arm in Karachi and was replaced by Boycott. That was interesting! Botham emerged as a world-class all-rounder.

I had my first taste of international captaincy, never having been in charge of a cricket team before in my life. No longer MCC, we were now England away as well as at home.

Were we right to stay with the Establishment or should we have joined up with World Series Cricket?

This book will provide some of the answers.

Bob Willis
October 2015

The Times They Are A Changing!

NOVEMBER 1977 and England departed from London on their winter tour to Pakistan, followed straight after by the second leg of the trip, to New Zealand. A gruelling and punishing schedule organised by the powers that be. Nothing has changed really, nearly forty years on!

The events prior to England's tour of Pakistan and New Zealand were to have a massive impact on the world of cricket. Twelve months earlier England had encountered a successful tour to India which was followed not only by the Centenary Test against Australia in Melbourne, but a victorious home Ashes series as well. The announcement of Kerry Packer's plans in May 1977 just before the commencement of that summer's Ashes series well and truly stirred the hornets' nest. 'The Times They Are A Changing' once sang Bob Dylan, hero of England fast bowler Bob Willis. Well, in the cricketing world, they most certainly were.

Who would have thought it was going to be a tour that contained so many incidents both on and off the pitch? Not only the riots that took place at the grounds amongst the political unrest in Pakistan, but history being created by Mudassar Nazar who scored the slowest ever Test century, a record that still stands to this day. The tour also saw New Zealand's first ever victory over England at the Basin Reserve in Wellington and the first time that Geoff Boycott had captained England in a Test after Mike Brearley was forced to return home with a broken arm. Promising Somerset all-rounder, 21-year-old Ian Botham, was included in an overseas tour party for the first time. Botham had already played two Tests at home in the summer, but this tour would see him score his maiden Test century. Also included in the squad were the uncapped Mike Gatting, Brian Rose, Geoff Cope and reserve keeper Paul Downton. The Test appearances of wicket-keeper Bob Taylor, plus spinners Phil Edmonds and Geoff Miller up to the time of departure, could be counted on one hand!

In some respects the tour was representing the dawning of a new era in English cricket. From the beginning of the 20th century, the MCC organised the England cricket team and, outside of Test matches, the touring England team officially played as the MCC. However, this tour would be the first overseas with the tourists playing every match as England. The Test series would be completed without several leading England and Pakistani Test players taking part, as they had defected to Packer's World Series Cricket.

At the time of these events in 1977, and the subsequent tour that England undertook that winter, I was a 14-year-old hooked by the game. I followed as much action as I could on television during the summer months. I re-enacted the matches outside with my friends in the street and on the playing fields, played hours of the Subbuteo Cricket game, kept comprehensive scrapbooks and devoured the newspapers for as much information as I could digest. When England's winter tours would take place I would listen to as much of the action as I could, like many youngsters of the time, with a transistor radio hidden under the bed covers and heading off to school the next day sleep deprived.

Living in the early 1970s in Tenby in West Wales, my only way of watching live cricket was following my father around whilst he played for Pembroke in the Pembrokeshire Cricket League. Well, I don't know how much cricket I actually watched as most of the time was spent playing cricket with the other children in a likewise position. After moving from Tenby in late 1974 it was not long before I was being taken by my father to my first games in the summer of 1975. It was really though in 1977 that I was being taken regularly to matches at grounds such as Sophia Gardens in Cardiff to watch my team, Glamorgan, and occasionally to other cricketing outposts at Worcester and Bristol. It was through watching County Championship and John Player League matches (and luckily a trip to Lord's to watch Glamorgan in that year's Gillette Cup Final) that I was able to witness close up many of the players that went on the winter Tour to Pakistan and New Zealand.

When researching my project I was amazed to find out that no one had ever written a book about the 1977/78 tour of Pakistan and New Zealand, especially considering that so much had occurred during it. And what's more, it just simply was a fascinating era in the history of the game.

This book is dedicated to the memory of my late father, Alan, who passed away in early 2014, and to whom I am grateful for introducing me to this great game. We spent many a happy day watching cricket together especially in my early years.

David Battersby
Cheltenham

Introduction

The Build-Up To Departure

THE impact of events in the cricket world during 1977 was massive, and no story of England's winter tour to Pakistan and New Zealand would be complete without turning back the clock twelve months and noting all that had taken place on and off the field.

The previous winter tour had seen England, for the first time in five ventures and the first since the Second World War, win on Indian soil. It was a decisive 3-1 series victory. England had gone 3-0 up in the series and the margins of victory had been convincing, winning by an innings and 25 runs, ten wickets and 200 runs. They were well led from the front by flamboyant and articulate skipper Tony Greig, who, aided by manager Ken Barrington, kept spirits high and made sure that a good discipline was maintained throughout. Senior players in the tour party, batsmen Mike Brearley and Keith Fletcher plus wicket-keeper Alan Knott, ensured that they were always on hand to contribute tactically. At times it had been a controversial tour, namely left-arm fast bowler John Lever and the historic 'Vaseline' incident! Lever was alleged to have rubbed Vaseline off his eye brows on to one side of the ball to make it swing better. He was later cleared of any wrongdoing. An historic aspect of the tour was that no other touring side had ever before in India clinched a series by winning the first three Tests! England showed no evidence of slackening on the tour and they returned home quite rightly triumphant.

A month after the tour to India had finished England departed for Melbourne and the Centenary one-off Test.

The first ever Test match had taken place at the Melbourne Cricket Ground between 15 and 19 March 1877 and was played without time restraints and four-ball overs. The Australians were victorious by 45 runs.

The Centenary Test was played close to 100 years later to the day, between 12 and 17 March 1977! It was to be the 800th Test match ever played, but this time with eight ball overs. England's team was made up from the squad that had toured India. Incredibly, after setting England 463 to win, Australia ended up winning the one-off Test by 45 runs, the same outcome as 100 years previously. The notable highlights had included a Bob Willis bouncer breaking Australian opener Rick McCosker's jaw, Rodney Marsh reaching his third century on the fourth day and becoming the first Australian wicket-keeper ever to make a Test century against England and the eccentric Derek Randall scoring 174 which was his debut Test century.

Unbeknown to all Kerry Packer, a media mogul billionaire, was planning his breakaway professional cricket competition, World Series Cricket, for his Australian television network. The series originated due not only to the widespread view that players were not paid sufficient amounts to make a living from cricket, but also because Packer wished to secure the exclusive broadcasting rights to Australian cricket, then held by the Australian Broadcasting Corporation (the ABC). After the Australian Cricket Board refused to accept Channel Nine's bid to gain exclusive television rights to Australia's Test matches in 1976, Packer set up his own secret signing agreements with leading Australian, English, Pakistani, South African and West Indian players.

Current England captain Tony Greig was not only convinced to sign up by Packer, but secretly acted as his agent in signing many top players from around the world. By the time of the end of the Centenary Test in Melbourne about two dozen players had in fact already signed on the dotted line. When the Australian tour team had arrived in England for the Ashes, thirteen of the seventeen members had already committed to Packer. The plans for World Series Cricket were inadvertently leaked to Australian journalists and the story broke on 9 May. There was uproar in the world of cricket! It seemed certain that all Packer players, as soon as they had played in World Series Cricket, would be banned from Test and first-class cricket.

The breaking news of Kerry Packer staging his World Series Cricket had rocked the game. The Australian Cricket Board refused to select players who had signed up to the rebel series, and as many of the Australian Test side had joined, the Australian squad was left without most of its star players. Fast bowler Jeff Thomson had originally signed up to play, but an existing media contract prevented him from joining so he remained free to lead the Australian bowling attack. Eventually all of the squad would go on to sign for Packer, the exceptions being Kim Hughes and Craig Serjeant.

The touring team was captained by Greg Chappell whilst Tony Greig was stripped of the England captaincy, but controversially kept his place in the side, which was now skippered by Mike Brearley.

England ended up dominating the Ashes Series. The first Test at Lord's, Brearley's first Test as captain, ended in a draw whilst England won the Second Test at Old Trafford by nine wickets. It was on to Trent Bridge for the third Test and a seven-wicket win put England 2-0 up. The fourth Test was held at Headingley and an eventful first day saw local hero Geoffrey Boycott score his hundredth hundred. It was a Test in which England destroyed Australia and won not only the game by an innings and 85 runs, but the Ashes as well. It was the first time England had won three Tests at home in a series against Australia since 1886. The fifth Test at The Oval was drawn; England had won the Ashes 3-0.

With the Ashes now over cricket entered an uncertain and unforeseen future as many of the top players in the world headed down under to participate in Kerry Packer's World Series Cricket. Included amongst them who had played for England in the last twelve months were Dennis Amiss, Tony Greig, Bob Woolmer, Alan Knott and Derek Underwood. Ex-England fast bowler John Snow, whose last Tests were in 1976 against the West Indies, also took part. Pakistan were also to have several players take part in the 'Circus' and were dubbed the 'Packerstanis'. These included Zaheer Abbas, Imran Khan, Majid Khan, Asif Iqbal and Mushtaq Mohammad.

England though had more pressing thoughts on their minds, a winter tour to Pakistan and New Zealand. The last Test of the summer always marked the announcement of the winter tour party. With the Packer players omitted, the announcement from the selectors at Lord's was eagerly anticipated.

Pakistan itself had become a hostile country. In March of 1977, Zulfikar Ali Bhutto's political Pakistan People's Party (PPP) won the election with 155 votes out of a possible 200, with the Pakistan National Alliance winning just 35. Rioting soon erupted throughout the country over allegations of vote-rigging by the PPP. Then on 5 July, Pakistan's Army led by General Zia-ul-Haq staged a military coup and seized power. Martial law was enforced and the Constitution was suspended. In September Zulfikar Ali Bhutto was arrested under martial law orders. General Zia had promised to hold National and Provincial Assembly elections within the next 90 days and to hand over power to the representatives of the nation. But then in the month prior to England's arrival in November, General Zia-ul-Haq decided to ban all opposition and all political activities! The Pakistan National Alliance policy had therefore been adopted, retribution first, elections later! Most certainly they were hostile times within the country and not the calmest of environments for England to travel around. In amongst all these political happenings, Pakistan had also celebrated its 30th year of independence on 14 August.

In the United Kingdom meanwhile other non-cricketing events had consisted mainly of the Silver Jubilee of Queen Elizabeth II and the emergence of the punk rock music scene, with debut albums released by The Sex Pistols and The Clash. Red Rum won the Grand National for the third time and in football, Liverpool won not only the league for a record tenth time, but the European Cup for the first time. Jim Callaghan, the Labour leader, was Prime Minister.

The announcement of the itinerary of the first leg of the tour to Pakistan had already been agreed before news of the tour party was released. The tour would start in the north in Pakistan's fourth-largest city, Rawalpindi in the Punjab, and gradually head south before ending in the port town of Karachi on the Arabian Sea, one of the largest cities in the world. England would play a three-match Test series in Lahore, Hyderabad and Karachi and three one-day internationals in Sahiwal, Sialkot and Lahore. The tour would kick off with three warm-up games, each consisting of three days each before the first Test. These would be against a BCCP Patron's XI in Rawalpindi, a United Bank XI in Faisalabad and a Governor's XI in Peshawar. There would also be a one-day tour game against Sind XI in Karachi plus two other three-day games sandwiched between the second and third Tests. These would be against the Habib Bank XI in Lahore and a Punjab XI in Bahawalpur. The tour would finish after the third Test in Karachi. All matches on the tour would consist of eight-ball overs.

The big talking point in the lead-up to the tour party being announced was who would fill the wicket-keeping positions now that Alan Knott had signed to World Series Cricket. Bob Taylor of Derbyshire was a nigh-on certainty to be the number one, but who would travel as his number two? David Bairstow, of Yorkshire, was the leading contender with Gloucestershire's Andy Stovold, due to his batting, a good outside bet. But when the tour party was announced the selectors astonished everyone by going for Kent's 20-year-old wicket-keeper Paul Downton. Chairman of selectors, Alec Bedser, said they had picked

Downton because 'he is the best prospect of the lot'. Downton had only played seven first-class matches and had leap-frogged other young prospects such as Nottinghamshire's Bruce French and Surrey's Jack Richards. Bedser said, 'We considered, and have an old England wicket-keeper in John Murray on our panel who knows a bit about the subject, that Downton is the most promising and could be the most brilliant wicket-keeper around. So we've put him in… giving youth a chance as we've so often been told to do.' Bedser continued, 'There are about 25 people who came very near to going, but we can only pick 16. Someone has to make the decisions.'

The selectors had frequently turned to older men in a crisis and the list of comebacks was as long as the list of meteoric promotions to the Test team is short. It became apparent that only John Murray of the selectors had seen Downton, but his recommendations were enough for his colleagues on the panel.

Downton had only made his Kent debut on 6 July which had followed the end of his first year at Exeter University. His second-year plans were going to have to be adjusted! Downton said, 'Obviously I had to make some very quick decisions this weekend. I got in touch with the university and arrangements are being made for me to start my second year next September. I was pretty amazed when I heard the news. It has not really hit me yet. I suppose my father has been my biggest influence, because he was a wicket-keeper and still plays for our local club, Sevenoaks Vine. It has also been a tremendous help being in the same county as Knott, who has been very kind to me, always ready to have a chat about wicket-keeping.'

Number one glove-man, Derbyshire's Bob Taylor, confessed that he knew nothing of Downton and had barely heard of him. Downton had made his debut against Surrey on 6 July at Maidstone and had made seven championship appearances dismissing 22 batsmen, 18 caught and four stumped. It later emerged that Downton's father, George, had also played for Kent, deputising on several occasions for Godfrey Evans.

Alan Knott responded to the news by saying, 'It's marvellous news to hear Paul has been selected. He looks such a natural wicket-keeper I think the earlier he gets his opportunity at this level the better it will be.'

Some had even touted for the young batsmen John Whitehouse (Warwickshire) and David Gower (Leicestershire) to be included, but the selectors decided instead to include the pugnacious, stocky, hard-hitting Mike Gatting of Middlesex and the focused Brian Rose of Somerset.

Twenty-seven-year-old Rose had been on the fringe of the Test team for some time. Gatting though had yet to make a first-class century and had still to learn how to compile a big innings. Gatting, like Downton, would have to alter his winter plans. Having had trials with Queens Park Rangers as a goalkeeper and with Watford as a left-back, the last winter had seen him turn out for Hendon – as a striker! Gatting had already been eyed up by the selectors early in 1977 having been included in the Prudential Trophy squad for the three-match one-day series against Australia, but did not play a game.

With Phil Edmonds as expected getting the chance to utilise his great potential, the only other real surprise in the party was the recall of Geoff Cope. The Yorkshire off-spinner had played well on the previous winter tour to India but had become disillusioned after not being selected for the Test matches.. Cope had been criticised in some quarters about a dubious action which he had attempted to remodel and what many had thought had put an end to his Test ambitions. Bedser explained, 'We have lost Underwood, who is such an accurate bowler, and we felt we had to have someone else who can put the ball where he wants it. Cope fills the bill. We are happy about his action. He was cleared by the adjudicating committee a long time ago and no umpire has reported him this season.'

Cope stated about his call-up, 'I haven't had as good a year as the last two seasons so I'm a bit surprised to be picked. The Indian trip was one of the best I've ever been on and with England in this sort of form this should be just as good.' Cope's team-mate at Yorkshire, Geoffrey Boycott, was rightly given the vice captaincy under Mike Brearley.

The tour party in full was:

Mike Brearley (Captain) (Middlesex – Age 35, 13 Tests)
Geoff Boycott (Vice Captain) (Yorkshire – Age 36, 66 Tests)
Ian Botham (Somerset – Age 21, 2 Tests)
Geoff Cope (Yorkshire – Age 30, 0 Tests)
Paul Downton (Kent – Age 20, 0 Tests)
Phil Edmonds (Middlesex – Age 26, 2 Tests)
Mike Gatting (Middlesex – Age 20, 0 Tests)
Mike Hendrick (Derbyshire – Age 28, 13 Tests)
John Lever (Essex – Age 28, 9 Tests)
Geoff Miller (Derbyshire – Age 24, 3 Tests)
Chris Old (Yorkshire – Age 28, 33 Tests)
Derek Randall (Nottinghamshire – Age 26, 10 Tests)
Graham Roope (Surrey – Age 31, 11 Tests)
Brian Rose (Somerset – Age 27, 0 Tests)
Bob Taylor (Derbyshire – Age 36, 1 Test)
Bob Willis (Warwickshire – Age 28, 29 Tests)
Manager: Ken Barrington

The 16-man squad had only played on average 12 tests each! And only three, Geoff Boycott, Chris Old and Bob Willis, had played more Tests than their ages. It was a fairly inexperienced side that set off from Heathrow in late November for the trip to Pakistan and New Zealand, a tour that would take three and a half months to complete! The players were to get £5,000 for the tour, a healthy amount due to Kerry Packer forcing up the market value and with Lord's desperately keen not to lose any more players to his rebel cricketing circus. The previous winter to India the players had got £3,000. On top of this players would also get £100 each for any previous tour. Test fees would now also increase, from £250 to £1,000. So those players that stayed away from Packer's World Series Cricket would now benefit as well!

1

A New Dawn – England take the Night Flight for Pakistan

That night, as improbable as England winning that day in Peshawar, the players celebrated their latest tour success by attending, in the unlikely setting of the North West Frontier, a performance of Romeo and Juliet *by the London Shakespeare Group!*

THE England party found themselves congregating at Heathrow Airport on 24 November on a chilly early winter evening. They would soon board the 13- hour flight to Pakistan via Istanbul with Ian Botham and Ken Barrington celebrating their 22nd and 47th birthdays respectively. The first tour game was to be held in Rawalpindi four days later against a BCCP Patron's XI.

Before they set off from Heathrow Airport, captain Mike Brearley said he was leading a team in a confident mood, but would not forecast how the team would fare. 'All the boys are looking forward to it very much, but it's difficult to make any prediction. We have a young side, but I'm sure everyone will pull their weight. We will do our best. Playing with Mike Gatting in the Middlesex team means that he holds no surprises to me. His main attributes are his strength and his running between the wickets. I've only seen Paul Downton once, but I was very impressed,' said Brearley.

Meanwhile, Wing Commander Imtiaz Ahmed, a former Test player and Pakistan's chairman of selectors, decided on using the first three, three-day tour matches as full scale trial matches for the hosts before the first Test began in Lahore on 14 December. In two of the games Wasim Bari, the new Test captain, was selected to play and every possible Pakistan candidate would be given a chance. For the first match against the BCCP Patron's XI eight full Test players were included in the squad of 14.

The day after arriving, England headed straight for the nets. The tour selectors, skipper Mike Brearley, vice captain Geoff Boycott, manager Ken Barrington and fast bowler Bob Willis, had tentatively selected sides for the first three matches whilst on the leg of the flight from Istanbul. 'We have to find our feet pretty quickly and think in terms of the combination for the Lahore Test. We haven't the time to experiment, and unhappily some are not going to get much of a chance. It is vital for us to get the middle-order batting sorted out, and the spin bowling,' stated manager Barrington. It was also noted by Barrington that, although the wicket in Rawalpindi for the first warm-up match had a reputation for spin, the Lahore track was one of the fastest in Pakistan.

England began nets placing a strong emphasis on fielding, an area in which they had been outstanding in the recent home series against Australia and the last winter trip to India. That first net session in Rawalpindi was to see Brearley telling young all-rounder Ian Botham that, in spite of his wickets the summer before, frankly, as an all-rounder, that the captain and the senior players considered him way below Chris Old and Geoff Miller. Brearley was later to state to Botham, 'To be brutally honest, at the tour's very first net practice at Rawalpindi, I wondered whether you should have made the trip at all, you made such a complete arse of yourself trying to hit those clever local spin bowlers out of the ground and all over the city. You could hardly lay a bat on them, you looked like a jokey village slogger out of his depth.' 'Thanks very much, skipper,' Botham had replied. 'At least you've told me where I stand.' More boldly, he added, 'For your information, that's how I always play nets, just a few swings to get my eye in.'

The first tour match was the three-day game against a BCCP Patron's XI at the Pindi Club Ground in Rawalpindi, starting on 30 November, the Patron being the State President, Fazal Elahi Chaudry.

Rain and a saturated pitch prevented any play from taking place until late on the first day, with a crowd of 6,000 patiently awaiting the sun to dry the pitch out at the Pindi Club Ground. Mike Brearley, who won the toss, decided against batting on a wicket that remained unpredictable. It was a decision he did not live to regret. The Patron's innings progressed at a snail's pace and in the sixty minutes of play possible before tea only 26 runs were put on the board without loss, the Patron's XI having been put into bat on a pitch that Fazal Mahmood, arguably their greatest ever bowler, stated he would have loved to have bowled on. It looked as though it had been dyed a darker shade in part!

Only 36 overs in two and a half hours' play were possible on day one, but it was enough time for Geoff Miller, bowling his off-breaks on a saturated pitch, to make his mark. He picked up the wickets of Mudassar Nazar, Haroon Rashid and Javed Miandad bowling over the wicket to record 3 for 14 from his six overs. Miller took wickets with his second and fourth balls and was the fifth bowler called upon by skipper Brearley, after the pace attack of Willis, Hendrick and Old and the left-arm spin of Edmonds had failed. The breakthrough came just after an hour and a half when Mudassar Nazar attempted to hit Miller to leg, but the ball went 12 feet up in the air off his pads and landed on the batsman's off stump, dislodging a bail.

It had been an unlucky day for Edmonds, who might have had two wickets early on before his bowling lapsed in length. Then, whilst fielding at short square leg, whilst Miller was bowling, he was hit on the left shoulder by Shafiq Ahmed. Painfully for Edmonds, worse was to follow. He was struck in the mouth from a shot by Javed Miandad, which resulted in a loosened tooth and bleeding inside the mouth. Edmonds bravely continued fielding, but wisely now retreated to orthodox square leg. The BCCP Patron's XI ended the day on 70 for 3 with opener Ahmed still there on 35 not out.

The next day saw Miller continue to bowl his off-breaks from the 'wet end' and he ended up with 6 for 62 as the Patron's XI were all out for 151. Shafiq Ahmed ended up top scoring with 52 and the only other innings of note was from Wasim Raja, the Test left-hander who played as an overseas professional for Ramsbottom in the Lancashire League. Raja heaved and cut, but on 29 finally fell to Willis when caught by Brearley. After several near misses, Willis and Old finally ended up with two wickets apiece.

England then suffered a nightmare on a bad pitch, which turned sharply with the ball keeping low. The batsmen were trapped on a pitch expertly exploited by Pakistan's Test bowlers. Having spent only three days in the nets in conditions not experienced by many, England were destroyed by Liaqat Ali's left-arm pace and Iqbal Qasim's left-arm orthodox spin. It all just proved too much. Ali, once a professional with Middlesbrough in the Yorkshire League, had the privilege of bowling Boycott between bat and pad for 2. The collapse saw the top order all dismissed cheaply, (Brearley for 0, Boycott 2, Rose 10, Randall 5, Roope 13) and England had crumbled to 44 for 6. Geoff Miller then showed some rear guard action with 21 not out, but England ended the day on a miserable 64 for 9. 'We had to bat on a wicket saturated at one end. It made batting very difficult' said Barrington after the day's play. 'Naturally we are disappointed to start this way, but at least things can only get better, and it will make some of the lads realise the task in front of them.'

England began the third and final day of this first tour match after declaring overnight, 87 runs in arrears of the Patron's XI score. The hosts then went about setting England a total and with mini-contributions from Rashid (22), Miandad (27) and Qadir (26 not out) declared on 118 for 6 off 41 overs with Mike Hendrick taking 2 for 20. Wasim Bari, the Patron's skipper, had decided to bat on until forty minutes before tea and that decision turned the game into an unintelligent exercise. A declaration an hour after lunch could have been just the thing to have produced a nail-biting finish.

Much criticism afterwards was aimed at left-arm spinner Phil Edmonds, who managed only 2 for 32 off ten overs and had failed to make a golden impression on the selectors. Afterwards, tour manager Barrington bluntly stated to Edmonds that he was not concentrating enough. Edmonds replied with honesty, 'Sometimes I feel I haven't given enough thought to a particular delivery.' Edmonds was too loose on a pitch where accuracy was essential. Overall, however, Barrington was not too displeased with the performance of the bowlers. 'At least they have got into the groove.'

England had been set a target of 206 to get in fifty-five minutes and 15 eight-ball overs and they reached 32 for 1 by the close of play. Spinner Iqbal Qasim produced a wicked ball to Boycott that reared sharply, producing a dolly catch to Mudassar Nazar.

'There was little to be learned about the batting on such a wicket. No batsman was ever set and all he could do was to take his life in his hands and graft. The home batsmen were just as troubled as we were,' Barrington concluded.

England travelled just over 300 kilometres south for their next game to Faisalabad, whose name had only been changed a few weeks previously from the name of Lyallpur. The game was another three-day match, this time against the United Bank

XI at the Iqbal Stadium. The first part of the journey by air to Lahore was delayed by four hours and, as there were no night landing facilities in Faisalabad, the rest of the 80-mile trip was undertaken by hastily acquired 'so-called' luxury coach!

The name change of the city of Faisalabad (the City of Faisal), located in the Punjab, was in honour of the late King Faisal of Saudi Arabia who was held in high regard in Pakistan. England by now were fully aware, after the chastening experience they had had in Rawalpindi, that the tour was not going to be an easy one.

The United Bank XI included in their line-up Mansoor Akhtar who earlier on in the year in February, when aged 19, had shared in an opening record-breaking stand of 561 for Karachi Whites against Quetta. England meanwhile decided to leave out Willis, Old and Taylor and select from the remaining 13 members of the squad, and would have to depend mainly on fast bowling and catching.

The last time England had visited Lyallpur was in 1969 under Colin Cowdrey. It had been a good pitch and with the city being situated further south saw the players experiencing impeccable weather.

Faisalabad, being the third-largest city in Pakistan behind Karachi and Lahore, would surely give the tourists more idea of what was to come on the tour in respect of hostile crowd reaction with the game being played in a large modern stadium.

In totally different conditions to the disastrous Rawalpindi match, and against a United Bank XI including only three recognised bowlers, Geoff Boycott and Brian Rose both found form scoring unbeaten centuries on day one. They hit an unbroken 225 for the second wicket as England closed the day on 284 for 1. It took Boycott forty minutes to get off the mark, but once he had got to his half-century he then hit seven of his 12 boundaries as he raised his tempo. Rose meanwhile, playing only his second overseas match, hit 12 fours and when Sadiq Mohammad, Gloucestershire's overseas player, bowled him a full toss, he hit it for six to reach three figures. Manager

Ken Barrington said, 'I thought Rose did extremely well and he seems to have settled down to new conditions with remarkable ease.'

The new-ball attack of Sikander Bakht and Aamer Hamid was too wayward to give Boycott any moments of anxiety. Boycott was on a mission to get to three figures and nothing was going to stop him after scoring two and eight in Rawalpindi. The only wicket to fall was that of captain Brearley for 18.

England decided to declare on their overnight total of 284 for 1 so Derek Randall, Graham Roope and the others missed out on vital batting practice on day two. England then set about their business in the field in a professional manner and saw the hosts declare late in the day with the score on 210 for 4, still 74 in arrears, with opener Sadiq joint top scoring with 53. The game saw the first glimpse of Ian Botham in action and he bowled impressively on an unresponsive slate-coloured pitch. Botham was rewarded with the wicket of Pakistan's number three, Haroon Rashid, caught by Brearley for 8. Khalad Irtiza then launched himself into the spin of Geoff Cope and as the ball hung forever in the blue sky, Botham made ground, steadied himself to take a great catch and Irtiza departed for 32.

Cope, in making his tour debut, ended with 2 for 53 off 20 overs and had dismissed both Sadiq and Khalid Irtiza with the first and eighth balls of his second spell. Test opener Talat Ali was the other wicket to fall, to Mike Gatting's second ball being dragged on from a bottom inside edge. Skipper Nasir Valika (53) and Mansoor Akthar (49) then put on 106 for the fifth wicket before Valika declared. Phil Edmonds still bowled without accuracy in taking 0 for 56 off eleven overs and there were strong cries from the media for Miller to be included as the solitary spinner for the forthcoming first Test in Lahore. England had twelve minutes to bat out and at the close were 11 for 0, giving makeshift openers Derek Randall and Graham Roope the chance to get some much needed batting practice on the last day.

Graham Roope certainly made the most of his chance on the final day hitting freely, making 102 not out, from the England total of 165 for 3. As soon as he reached three figures, Mike Brearley declared, setting the United Bank XI 240 in two hours. The match petered out and was abandoned as a draw midway through the last 15 overs with the hosts on 58 for 2. The match had seen none of the tourists' other batsmen profiting from time at the crease, Randall falling for 26, Gatting for 6 and Botham for a duck. Spinner Geoff Cope picked up the two wickets (taking 2 for 19 off his eight overs) and finished the match with his head held high. Ken Barrington was at last pleased to see left-arm spinner Phil Edmonds record figures of 0 for 6 off his nine overs.

The lifeless Iqbal Stadium pitch had provided no assistance to the bowlers and was ideal for a batsman looking for a big score. The large number of enthusiasts who had turned up to watch the match strengthened Faisalabad's claim as a Test centre. With the match drawn, England were still in much need of match practice and returned north to take on the Governor's XI in Peshawar.

England travelled up to the North West Frontier for their third and final three-day tour match, prior to the first Test, playing against the North West Frontier Province Governor's XI at the Club Ground in Peshawar. Peshawar had become one of the prime cities west of the River Indus and the capital of the Khyber-Pakhtunkhwa region, with the legendary Khyber Pass only an hour away by car.

This was to be England's fourth visit to the ground since their first tour of Pakistan back in 1961/62. The last, though, in February 1973 had seen, due to the weather, the whole three-day game against the Governor's XI being abandoned without a ball being bowled!

The Club Ground in Peshawar held special memories for England captain Mike Brearley. Whilst still at Cambridge University, he was chosen to captain the MCC Under-25s on their 1966/67 tour of Pakistan. It was a hugely successful trip for

Brearley who ended the tour scoring 793 runs from six matches with an average of 132. During the match against the North Zone at Peshawar in February 1967 Brearley hit 312 in 330 minutes, an innings that included 46 fours and three sixes. This was to remain Brearley's highest first-class score. Also on that tour he scored 223, against the Pakistan Under-25 side in Dacca. The three under-25 Tests were all drawn.

England batted first against the Governor's XI with Boycott and Brearley recording a century stand against accurate pace bowling from Hasan Jamil, Ehteshamuddin and Parvez Mir. Brearley, returning to the scene of his triple century, was first to go, bowled for 57 by Abdul Raqib. Boycott though was as attentive as ever and ended the day 115 not out. After Rose was run out for 12 and Randall bowled by Wasim Raja for 15, Roope then joined Boycott, and the pair put on 112 for the fourth wicket. Roope attractively attacked the tiring bowlers, and at stumps was 63 not out, with England declaring on 285 for 3 off 76 overs at the close of play.

The match in Peshawar saw Essex left-arm swing bowler John Lever play his first game of the tour. Lever did not disappoint, adding fire and variety to the attack. On a pitch moistened by dew, which made the ball skim through, a highly satisfactory bowling performance by England on day two saw them dismiss the North West Frontiers Governor's XI for 127, in just under four hours.

Lever, having missed the match in Faisalabad through illness, produced instant success, bowling opener Agha Zahid for a duck with his third ball. An excellent seventy-five-minute spell saw him also remove Taslim Arif's middle stump with a swinging yorker. The Governor's XI was primarily a Pakistan second team and included former Test captain Saeed Ahmed, brother of Younis Ahmed, who last played for Pakistan in 1973. Sadly, only one local player, Farrukh Zaman, was included in the team. Petty politics within Pakistan cricket had dictated who should or shouldn't be included. Ahmed was given a torrid time, particularly by Bob Willis who delivered a hostile spell.

Saeed lost his off stump to the last ball of Willis's second over. Once Lever and Willis had softened up the batsmen, Chris Old stepped in to take 3 for 11 in nine overs, removing Pervez, Raqib and Ehteshamuddin. Geoff Miller continued a good start to the tour with his off-spin, removing Azmat Rana and last man Zaman to finish with 2 for 23. Lever ended with 3 for 49 and Willis 2 for 13. It was now an encouraging dilemma for the selectors to have, with Lever and Mike Hendrick competing for the Test place. England finished the day on 53 for 1 after not enforcing the follow-on and batted through the final eighty minutes of the day with the only wicket to fall that of Brian Rose for 21.

News during the day broke through of Pakistan's inquiries of their Packer players to possibly play in the Tests, to an astonished Ken Barrington. He said, 'It seems inconceivable to hear this less than a week before the first Test. The attitude of the team is that, if Pakistan want them, then let them come.'

Rain through the night meant play started half an hour late at the start of the third and final day and a turning pitch gave no help to England's batsmen. They added 53 to their overnight total before declaring on 122 for 3, losing Derek Randall for 57 and with Ian Botham ending on 22 not out. Randall played throughout the morning before advancing down the pitch and falling victim to Saeed Ahmed's off-spin. Randall played some fine strokes and an innings of merit. Botham, meanwhile, was in need of batting practice after having not made a run on the tour to date. After being dropped at slip second ball off Wasim Raja, arguably the best leg-spinner in the world, Botham had got that hard-earned practice before Brearley declared.

Saeed Ahmed had scarcely played cricket for five years and it was something of a mystery as to why he was included in this game. He was in for another torrid time from Bob Willis. Willis, once sighting Ahmed at the crease, bowled faster and shorter. It was Lever though that got Ahmed out, playing on the back foot when on 3 and finding the only fielder, Derek Randall, in front of the wicket on the off side. The Governor's XI had been routed for 68 and England had won by 212 runs. Lever had taken three wickets with two apiece for Willis and Old. Lever, in taking his first wicket in the Governor's XI second innings, reached his 700th wicket in first-class cricket. With a highly satisfactory mission accomplished and the redoubtable Boycott in fine form it was hard to see England losing the first Test in Lahore.

Pakistan's national sports publication *Sportstimes* looked back on the game and stated, 'It was no match indeed. Nothing more than an occasion for the visitors to get a lot of practice on a fine wicket in preparation for the opening Test at Lahore and, of course, an opportunity for them to register their first win of the tour. For all practical purposes, the NWFP Governor's Eleven was nowhere in the game and had it been left to some of the local chaps, the result would not have been that bad – if bad is the proper word for the sort of beginner-like cricket the home team played.' The local Peshawarites who had turned up to watch the encounter had been hard done by. They had witnessed a bad exhibition of cricket in return for the heavy investment of Rs. 1.50 lakh. The comeback of former Test captain Saeed Ahmed had been a gross disappointment. He contributed just one wicket and three runs.

That night, as improbable as England winning that day in Peshawar, the players celebrated their latest tour success by attending, in the unlikely setting of the North West Frontier, a performance of *Romeo and Juliet* by the London Shakespeare Group!

2

England take on Pakistan at the Gaddafi Stadium

The comic genius, Derek Randall, was at it again. He defused the situation of the pitch invasion when Miandad had reached his half-century by running across from cover and embracing the batsman Pakistani-style by planting a kiss on his cheek.

ENGLAND headed back down south into the Punjab to begin preparations for the first Test at the Gaddafi Stadium in Lahore. Two days prior to the start of the Test, England's net session took place at the Gymkhana Ground. However, only one net was available for the 16 tourists which did not please the manager, Ken Barrington. Barrington was then told at lunchtime that his request for a switch to the Gaddafi Stadium, where the Pakistanis were using two nets, had been turned down. He hot-footed it over to the stadium where it was finally agreed that they could use the facilities, which should have been a matter of courtesy for visiting teams.

The 38-strong Pakistan squad had been encamped at the stadium for weeks, but that squad had by now been whittled down to 19 from whom the Test team was to be selected plus the Packer players Majid Khan, Mushtaq Mohammad, Zaheer Abbas and Imran Khan. The four defectors had been included on the instructions of the president of the Pakistan board, Mohammad Hussain Chaudi. Wasim Bari, the captain, said he would be happy to have the four players included. He went on to state that as for the players left out, they would have a chance in the not-too-distant future.

The uproar of whether Pakistan would include the Packer players to play or not might not have come to anything anyway as the pitch was looking good, and it was predicted that it would have to take one team to bat really badly to lose the Test.

England began practising the day before the Test at the Gaddafi Stadium, but it turned into a fiasco. Manager Barrington, after the lengths he had been to to use the stadium, was appalled at the state of the wickets that had been provided. It wasn't long before he found himself complaining to the Pakistan board. After just two balls of the net session, which resulted in Mike Gatting getting hit, the tour party returned to the Gymkhana ground to continue practising in the one net available.

'The wickets at the stadium were exceptionally dangerous,' said Barrington. 'I shall ask the board to prepare better facilities for the future.'

The day before the Test, England named their team and the main news story was of the inclusion of Geoff Cope, the 30-year-old off-break bowler from Yorkshire. It was hard for Cope to conceal his emotions as having been overlooked on the previous winter's tour to India, he also had to overcome the stigma of a long struggle over his bowling action. Twelve months previously, he also had to fly home from the Indian trip due to the death of his father. Cope said, 'It was a lot for me to take in. I had to think of my father, who would have been especially proud at this moment, the crossroads crisis of my career, and the two men who saw me through – Johnny Wardle and Geoff Boycott.'

Cope had been suspended for the second half of the 1972 season because of doubts about his action, but was cleared the following season by the Test and County Cricket Board sub-committee on the evidence of films. Ex-England and Yorkshire slow left-arm spinner Johnny Wardle was the man to put it all right. 'Johnny spent months working with me. I owe a great deal to Johnny and Geoff and nothing would give me greater pleasure than to pay them back with success in the Test,' said Cope.

Cope's chance came with fitness doubts about the bed-ridden room-mates Ian Botham and Mike Hendrick who both went down with amoebic dysentery. Cope's room-mate on the tour was Somerset left-handed batsman Brian Rose who was also selected in the side to make his debut. Rose had already scored 110 not out in Faisalabad and the last summer had also seen him hit five centuries including one against the Australians.

Captain Mike Brearley dryly commented about Pakistan including the Packer players in their squad by saying, 'One of the purposes of the get-together is to discuss the opposition. But this time it is difficult to know who we are playing against. I have no access to the situation of the Packer men, but if we went through the possibilities it would be the longest team discussion on record. I am hopeful we can win.' The England party relaxed the night before with the traditional dinner.

As Wasim Bari and Mike Brearley headed out for the toss it was apparent that the plans to play the four 'Packerstanis' was a futile exercise. The Pakistan board said as much in a released statement, but even up to the eve of the match the public were still being told there was a possibility of them playing, even though there was never ever any chance of it happening. Bari won the toss and elected to bat. The Pakistani skipper Bari was also an excellent wicket-keeper. Many years later in 2015 Geoffrey Boycott was to comment that Bari was 'a crackerjack of a keeper, had beautiful hands'.

The day turned out to be tiresome and boring for pretty much all concerned. The 20,000 crowd mainly amused themselves by baiting the police with orange peel. Pakistan plodded along and finished the day on 164 for 2 off 63 overs. Opener Mudassar Nazar reached the close on 52 not out with Haroon Rashid on 84. The day really became a stalemate between the two sides as Pakistan's batting crawled along. Nazar, son of national coach Nazar Mohammad, remained patient all day long. He got to his 50 after 170 minutes and ended the 300-minute day on 52! Powerful strokeplayer Haroon Rashid was more enterprising, reaching his fifty in two hours. England had broken through the opening partnership after an hour and forty-three minutes when Sadiq was lbw to Geoff Miller's third ball for 18. Shafiq Ahmed, batting at three, was then caught by Rose, off Old, without scoring. Nazar and Rashid then put on 115 before the close of play. Cope had bowled thoughtfully and ended the day with 0 for 23 off 12 overs, and was unlucky not to have had Rashid out when deceiving the batsman when he was on 46. The ball delivered by Cope brushed Rashid's pads as he moved to play the shot, and, with the batsman leaving his crease, he luckily saw the ball fall just wide of Bob Taylor, who was unable to gather it in time. Rashid regained his ground to avoid being stumped.

The second day was eventful to say the least! Mudassar Nazar finally completed his century in 557 minutes (nine hours and seventeen minutes), to break the record for the slowest century in Test cricket by twelve minutes. The previous record holder had been South Africa's Jackie McGlew, who had reached his hundred against Australia at Durban in January 1958. Nazar reached his century off 419 balls, which is a record that still stands. Nazar's innings of 114 lasted nine minutes short of ten hours and was ended when he was caught and bowled by Geoff Miller. Nazar's dismissal took the score to 329 for 4. His snail-like innings was as drab as they came, but credit should be given to him for his amazing powers of concentration. When Nazar had reached 99 twenty-five minutes before tea some spectators believed he had reached his hundred and they had invaded the pitch to congratulate him. The local Punjab police reserve chased most of them off the ground but, unwisely, stayed on the field.

The increasing taunts and growing tension erupted when a more formidable group of the crowd jumped over the fences and forced the England fielders to the dressing room. One of the invaders was set upon by the police and this resulted in running fights between the police and fans. Incensed by the beatings and kickings, which took place in full view of the 20,000 crowd, the mob chased the rapidly retreating police across the pitch. As soon as they had re-assembled, the police counter-charged without success and were again driven back with even stumps used as weapons. Bricks, bottles, fruit and debris were hurled at them as they retreated to a position in front of the dressing rooms with four policemen even finding refuge in the England dressing room. During all the chaos the umpires, Amanullah Khan and Aslam Khokhar, wisely decided that an early tea be taken. Insults against the police were shouted until peace was restored with the intervention of Wasim Bari, the home skipper.

A bizarre scenario soon followed, as some of the rioters then decided to clear the playing area of the debris! Things calmed a little when Ken Barrington and Mike Brearley returned with officials to examine the pitch. England agreed to a restart straight after tea, which meant only twenty-five minutes of play were lost. Ken Barrington said, 'Pakistan apologised and made it abundantly clear that the disturbance was not directed at the players. Despite the fact that hundreds of feet went over the pitch there were no visible signs of damage. We felt extremely sorry for the officials and we accepted their apologies.'

Mike Gatting, meanwhile, watched Nazar's slow century from the commentary box and had a good view of the pitch invasion, brick-throwing and a section of the crowd's running fights with the police.

Other pitch invasions took place when Nazar reached his hundred and Javed Miandad his fifty, but these were good-natured. The comic genius, Derek Randall, was at it again. He defused the situation of the pitch invasion when Miandad had reached his half-century by running across from cover and embracing the batsman Pakistani-style by planting a kiss on his cheek.

There was a fear of other rioting taking place at the game, with the genuine cricket fan hoping that there would be no repeat of the 1969 third Test in Karachi, which was abandoned on the third day after repeated disturbances. In that instance the police were inept and provocative. Haroon Rashid, having put on 180 for the third wicket with Nazar, finally fell for 122, caught and bowled by John Lever. Day two ended with Pakistan on a healthy 360 for 5.

The third day's play was once again seriously affected by rioting, which this time was more serious and put the whole of the tour in jeopardy.

Police fired tear gas to disperse a flare-up, apparently caused by the appearance of Nusrat Bhutto, wife of the former Prime Minister, who was standing trial in the city at the same time as the Test match.

The trouble started when Bhutto, along with her daughter Benazir, were refused permission to enter the ground by the main gate for which they had tickets. They then went to the women's stand, but found it locked. A section of the 35,000 crowd standing on top of the enclosure began chanting insults, which resulted in chairs being smashed, bottles and stones thrown and a section of wire fencing, separating spectators from the dressing-room section of the ground, being broken down as the crowd began trying to get in. The crowd even began the burning of a bus which was parked inside the ground. A piece of flying debris hit Nusrat Bhutto on the head which resulted in her having to have three stitches. When the police waded in, all hell broke loose.

Once the trouble had started, the players had raced from the field for the dressing room, with rubbish and seats raining down all around them.

The police had now gathered in force in front of the women's enclosure. One man who had thrown a bottle was carried, struggling, onto the playing field by the police and a fire was started by the side of the section of the ground where the women sat. The bricks that marked the boundary were turfed up by sections of the crowd and thrown at the police. After making a stand in the middle of the pitch the police were soon forced back.

How could England carry on playing in a country that was in such a highly sensitive political situation? The scenes were reminiscent of that of Colin Cowdrey's tour of 1969 and the riot in Karachi.

The English players were now locked inside the dressing room, even barricading themselves in, putting chairs against the windows, standing, armed with bats in hand as the crowd outside unfurled a barrage of aggressive shouting. Soon they could make out that the crowds were not after the players, just the police! It didn't take long however for police reinforcements to arrive in considerable numbers, with peace finally being restored.

On the pitch, controversial drama had unravelled with debutant Geoff Cope being denied a hat-trick. Cope dismissed both Abdul Qadir and Sarfraz Nawaz with consecutive balls with Iqbal Qasim then caught at slip by Mike Brearley. Cope and England celebrated as Iqbal was given out by umpire Amanullah Khan. Brearley though had an element of doubt about his catch and called him back. He said afterwards that it was an instinctive grab and he was not certain he had held a clean catch! Cope ended with 3 for 102 off 39 overs. Cope gave an interview to John Ward in 2003 that appears on the Cricket Archive website. Cope recalled that, 'Iqbal Qasim came in, a little left-hander. I chose to go round the wicket and obviously we put men round the bat, "Brears" (Mike Brearley, the captain) at first slip, Graham Roope, Bob Willis, "Both" (Ian Botham) all round the bat. I just bowled it right and it was magic really; it just turned a fraction and bounced, and "Iqqie" nicked it.

Brears just dived to his left and caught the ball about a foot off the ground, landing in front of Roopey and Willis. Iqqie just looked up the wicket at me, nodded, said, "Well bowled"; the umpire went bananas, shaking hands and saying, "I've never seen a hat-trick before, well bowled." And ironically this was on my debut. Twelve months previously, on the same ground, Peter Petherick of New Zealand had just done the first hat-trick ever on debut, so it would have been 12 months to the day and it would have been a unique place in history. But Mike in landing got a lot of gravel on the back of his hand. Iqqie left the field and all the lads were up there when suddenly Brears started saying, "I'm going to bring him back, I don't think I caught it cleanly." All the lads around him were adamant he had caught it a foot off the ground, but he said, "No, for the best interests of this series I'm going to bring him back." So he brought him back – and for the best interests of the series, six of us were lbw in our first innings. It happened, but it was a moment of disappointment because something like that on a Test debut is very special. As somebody once said, "if bad luck hadn't been invented, we'd have had none at all!"'

Geoff Miller coincidentally, like Cope, also took 3 for 102, but off two less overs. Pakistan declared on 407 for 9.

Play was abandoned after the riot took hold, fifty-five minutes before the scheduled close with England 85 for 2. With the score on 53, Brearley was sent back by Boycott and was given run-out following a throw from deep point by Wasim Raja. Brearley felt he was comfortably home. Brian Rose then lost his wicket a run later, when umpire Amanullah controversially gave him out, leg before, to Sarfraz from a rising ball. Ken Barrington reflected on the day's events on the pitch stating, 'It is a fascinating struggle. England might yet have to fight hard to avoid defeat.' A lot depended on Boycott who ended play on 38 not out.

After the much needed rest day for all concerned, the ground on the fourth day was heavily policed, but only 5,000 silent and subdued spectators turned up to watch. As play got under way there were at least ten police, including the riot squad, to every spectator. The police were also sitting in groups in the stadium at strategic points. Plain clothes men also sat among the spectators. With the wicket that had been produced, another mundane day of cricket took place.

England lost Derek Randall and Graham Roope to bad shots and it was left to Boycott to drop anchor. In fact Boycott's fifty came in 290 minutes, which was twenty minutes slower than Mudassar Nazar's had been at the halfway stage to the slowest century on record. Who knows how long it would have taken Boycott if he had not been dismissed when on 63 and after seven and three-quarter hours at the crease.

Boycott was beaten when playing back to the orthodox turn of Iqbal Qasim's left-arm spin and was bowled. An impressive 13-over spell saw Qasim remove Boycott, Roope and Chris Old.

The day, however, belonged to Derbyshire's Geoff Miller who, with fellow county team-mate Bob Taylor, added 83 up until the close with Miller 71 not out and Taylor on 32. Using his feet against the spin of Qasim and the leg-breaks and googlies of Abdul Qadir, Miller also attentively stopped the good ball in an intelligent batting display. England ended the day on 245 for 6, still 162 behind.

Geoff Miller started the final day on 71 and was attempting to become the first England player to score a maiden first-class century in a Test since Billy Griffith in 1948. The overnight 245 for 6 soon became 253 for 9 with the loss of Taylor for 32 and both John Lever and Geoff Cope for ducks. Last man Bob Willis joined Miller, who was now on 79, and remained his staunch partner for an hour and a half. But then on 14 Willis, having resisted both pace and spin, played forward to a googly from Abdul Qadir, scraped the ground with his bat as he missed the ball and saw it fly off his pads to Qasim at backward short leg and was controversially given out caught!

England were all out for 288 and Miller was left stranded on 98 not out having batted with a cold and streaming eyes for six hours. 'We were all sick for Geoff that he did not get those two runs, but his performance showed that he is now a very mature player,' said Ken Barrington.

Pakistan closed on 106 for 3 in their second innings, a lead of 225, with the final day of the first Test predictably ending in a draw. England had now drawn nine out of ten Tests in the country.

Meanwhile an order was placed on Miss Benazir Bhutto, daughter of the former Prime Minister, putting her under house arrest due to her appearance at the Test match on day three, which, it claimed, had resulted in arson, loss of property and a danger to human life.

Unfortunately, the Lahore Test match would always be remembered for the wrong reasons.

Some reporters thought that Miss Bhutto's appearance at the Test looked like a deliberately provocative attempt to take advantage of a large crowd, at a time when public gatherings of more than a few dozen people were not normally allowed in Pakistan. Miss Bhutto, meanwhile, had even recently been president of the Oxford Union. One wonders if she had strolled to The Parks to watch Oxford University in action whilst at Oxford.

The *Sportstimes* publication in Pakistan summed up the Test. 'For the sake of conventional cricket, which needs all the help and encouragement it can get after Packer's uninvited intrusion, I urge the authorities to aim for faster pitches in the two remaining Tests in Hyderabad and Karachi. Another drawn series is a singularly unwelcome prospect, but I see no alternative unless something is done about the pitches. Winning the toss and building up an almost inevitable safety total – that is an immunity from defeat – is a boring exercise and does cricket no good in Pakistan.'

Mudassar Nazar still holds the Test record for that slowest century in Lahore which took 557 minutes. Nazar is currently (as at the beginning of March 2012) a batting coach at the ICC Global Cricket Academy in Dubai. Speaking during the 2012 Test series between Pakistan and England in the United Arab Emirates, Nazar was asked if he was proud of his batting record.

He replied, 'No, I shy away from it and cringe when people bring it up.' Was he always a slow batsman? 'No. I wasn't, but the point was Pakistan had lost a lot of their back-up players. Majid, Mushtaq, Zaheer, Imran, they weren't playing, but England had retained a lot of their great players like Boycott and Bob Willis. Our main aim, I was told, was that we were not going to lose this Test match and the Pakistan Cricket Board were adamant that the back-up players would remain out forever, but there was a hue and cry from Pakistan to get their top players back. So their main aim was that we would not lose this Test match.

'Just before tea, I remember going down the track to slog Geoff Miller. Wasim Bari, the captain, sent out the gloves to say "play for the team not yourself", music to my ears. I got 48 at tea-time. Bob Willis was bowling first ball after tea. I smashed him through the covers for four so I thought right, I'll get to grips with him, start scoring and at the end of the day's play I was still on 52! I was very happy to be on 52 overnight and start from scratch the day after. I just wanted to get a hundred. My second Test match and I went on to get a hundred. I don't remember what the England bowlers were doing, but Bob Willis was a quality bowler. Geoff Miller, Geoff Cope and John Lever were playing. They had a decent bowling attack. It was a fantastic batting pitch. Later on in the years if I'd been batting I would have got a hundred a lot quicker, on this pitch (in Dubai) against that bowling attack.

'I met a girl in Dhaka about ten years ago, I was coaching there, she was talking about cricket. I said did you ever play cricket? She said "No". "Did you ever watch cricket?" and she said "I watched it only once". I said "when?" She said "When you got your slowest hundred." She never came to watch again!' Nazar said laughing!

Pakistan journalist Mehdi Qizilbash wrote at the time of Nazar's innings, 'There is a big section of cricket fans who are critical over his dog-trot approach: but we must not forget that he is cast in a classical mould. He is just like Hanif and Boycott, all concentration and treating every ball on its merit.

Most Pakistani fans I've met regard Mudassar's batting dull and boring. Maybe they are right, but it must be remembered that while Mudassar occupies the crease, Pakistan has a good chance of piling up a good score.' Qizilbash went on to add, 'It is a credit to one so young to notch up the slowest-ever century in a Test, but he should not make it a habit like Boycott or Hanif. He should adapt himself as the situation demands. I'm sure he is capable of doing it as he has the strokes and the guts to brighten up things. Only time will tell how he shapes.'

Meanwhile Pakistan's vice captain, fast bowler Sarfraz Nawaz, in the aftermath of the Lahore Test, dramatically headed for London after a row with the Pakistan board over an air fare and his professional fees relating to him playing in the series. He was adamant that, unless the dispute was settled, he would not play in the second Test beginning in Hyderabad on 2 January.

Sarfraz, the Northamptonshire fast bowler, sent a letter to the Pakistan Board of Control stating that he had left London to travel to Pakistan 'to serve his beloved country' convinced his air fare and playing fees would be amicably settled. However, events proved this not to be the case. He also stated that he was never consulted in the selection of the team which was unheard of for a vice captain. It was understood Sadiq Mohammad (Gloucestershire) and Javed Miandad (Sussex) had had their air fares paid.

All three players were employed by the United Bank, but since the pay row which had resulted in pay rises for several players in the previous year, professionalism in Pakistan had been abolished. Test players now got roughly £300 per Test.

England continued to practise at the Gymkhana Club in Lahore in preparation for their next tour match, the first one-day international in Sahiwal on 23 December. Two days before the game England manager Ken Barrington was at last happy with the performance of left-arm spinner Phil Edmonds in the nets. 'I have never seen him bowl better. He controlled his length and direction and spun the ball a lot.' The one-day international was to be played over 35 overs, with each over consisting of eight balls and the bowlers limited to a 15-pace run-up.

England decided to rest vice captain Geoff Boycott for the international, giving the others some much needed batting practice. Boycott spent the day busily organising nets at the Gymkhana Club in Lahore at a time in the year of Muharram ul Haram, when no music is played and the foreign permit hotel bars remain closed. Ken Barrington publicly commented about Boycott on the trip. 'He is quite the most dedicated cricketer in my experience. He works everything out. When he's out, he comes back in the dressing room and sits by himself for twenty minutes reasoning how and why he got out. Nobody thinks it fitting to talk to him. He has the team at heart, and restricts himself in his batting because he is aware of the responsibility he carries, and everyone here wants to claim the honour of getting him out.'

Barrington meanwhile was not impressed with the way in which Derek Randall and Graham Roope lost their wickets in the Test: 'They played haphazard shots at crucial stages.'

The squad, inevitably, were encountering a depressing period of the tour with hotel restrictions in place producing boredom, and sickness doing the rounds, not forgetting homesickness and bad umpiring decisions. Boycott himself was philosophical. 'I tell 'em it's always better than working down the pits. It is better for your world to fall down with a bad decision than for a roof of a mine to fall down on top of you,' he said.

Meanwhile in Lahore, a judicial inquiry had begun under the instructions of the federal government regarding the rioting that had taken place on the third day of the Test at the Gaddafi Stadium.

England were using the first one-day international in Sahiwal primarily as batting practice and were due to field a weakened 'second Test XI' against the Habib Bank XI in the next tour match in Lahore beginning on Boxing Day.

England, having rested Boycott, decided to select Brian Rose to open with Mike Brearley, with Chris Old batting at number four. Derek Randall (who had now recovered from sickness), Graham Roope and Ian Botham would follow in the order and all were in desperate need of batting practice. A match against a local side was also being considered. Youngsters Mike Gatting and Paul Downton were also chosen as they had to date only played in one three-day tour game.

Manager Ken Barrington commented about the problems of giving everyone a game. 'The itinerary is such that it is a problem to give everyone sufficient cricket. But those who are missing out in Pakistan will have better chances in New Zealand in the second part of the overseas tour.

'The Shiawal match is a real chance for the players who haven't had much cricket on the tour so far. It's up to them to take it,' said Barrington.

No doubt, Phil Edmonds was one Barrington was thinking of, a player England would like to see bring much needed variety to their bowling attack and whose good arm in the field would be welcomed as well.

Meanwhile, Pakistan would be without fast bowler Sarfraz Nawaz, because of his ongoing dispute with the Pakistan Cricket Board and Haroon Rashid, man of the match in the first Test, who was suffering from a leg injury.

The Zafar Ali Stadium in Sahiwal, venue for this first one-day international on 23 December, was rammed to the rafters with a crowd of 15,000 locked in and thousands being turned away. This was the first England trip overseas where one-day internationals were included on a tour itinerary.

Sahiwal, whose main industry was cotton and textile, began life as a small village called Montgomery located on the Karachi to Lahore railway line in 1865, and was named after the Lieutenant-Governor of the Punjab. In 1966 Montgomery was renamed Sahiwal and had become the biggest city between Lahore and Multan. This was the first time a one-day international had been played at the Zafar Ali Stadium. In fact to date the only other international game to be played at the ground was 11 months later, in November 1978, against India.

The MCC, however, had played an aborted three-day game at the stadium during the 1969 tour against the West Pakistan Governor's XI when the hosts were 87 for 1. The match had been abandoned, after 25 overs, due to political demonstrations against the military regime. England would return in 1987 for a three-day, drawn, tour game against a Punjab Chief Minister's XI.

One-day internationals had begun back in January 1971 with the hastily arranged match between England and Australia in Melbourne. This match in Sahiwal was the 45th in the history of the game and only England's 26th! England had played Pakistan only twice before, losing both games in 1974, at Trent Bridge and Edgbaston. Could it be third time lucky? However, this was just Pakistan's ninth one-day international!

Pakistan skipper Wasim Bari won the toss and elected to bat. After just eight minutes, opener Sadiq was bowled by Ian Botham for 2. Nazar was then run out for 20 and Shafiq Ahmed (29) was bowled by Geoff Miller: the hosts were in a spot of bother at 63 for 3. Javed Miandad then came to the crease and he took the bull by the horns, scoring an inspired 77 not out, hitting two sixes and three fours. England were to rue Mike Hendrick, fielding at long off, dropping Miandad off the bowling of Chris Old, when Miandad was on 2. With an able partner in Hasan Jamil, the pair plundered 50 runs off the final three overs, which were bowled by Hendrick, Botham and Old. Jamil though fell to the penultimate ball of the innings, caught by debutant Paul Downton off Botham for 20. The wicket gave Botham his third and he ended with excellent figures of 3 for 39 from his seven eight-ball overs. Pakistan's total of 208 for 6 off their 35 overs was a challenging one.

England got off to a good start. Openers Mike Brearley and Brian Rose put on 66 for the first wicket before Brearley went for 30. Mike Gatting was run out for 17 but Rose, without being convincing, batted through 26 overs before falling for 54 when caught and bowled by the leg-spin of Wasim Raja. Chris Old was unlucky seven runs later, as with the score on 134, he fell leg before to Parvez Mir after snicking a ball onto his pads. Derek Randall (35) and Graham Roope (29) accelerated things at the right time, both hitting two sixes, three of them out of the small ground. Roope was immediately rewarded with rupees from spectators and doffed his cap in acknowledgement. Things were progressing well and a tight finish was on the horizon. With ten overs left, 90 runs were required, then 48 off five and finally 28 in three. Soon the last over arrived and England now required ten runs off eight balls, and a lot depended on how 22-year-old Ian Botham would react to such pressure.

The last over was to take fifteen minutes and at one point skipper Brearley had to intervene to point out to the umpires that the scoreboard had dropped from 205 to 204 and then to 203. This had happened after Phil Edmonds was run out off the fourth ball, going for a third run on an overthrow. The scoreboard operators thought that the batsmen were only allowed one run instead of two. Once the confusion had been sorted, England now needed four off four. New batsman Miller snatched a bye, but Botham then played defensively next ball and three runs were required off two balls. The penultimate ball of the over from the left arm of Liaqat Ali saw Botham drive for a couple of runs, and the scores were now level. Skipper Wasim Bari consulted with team-mates and endeavoured to spread his field over every inch of the ground. Pakistan had lost six wickets to England's seven, so the tie would give the hosts victory. With Pakistan's fielders placed in a defensive ring, Liaqat began his run up as the whole crowd began making a tremendous din as they roared him in. Botham stood composed at the crease as Liaqat bowled the ball exactly where the batsman wanted it, selecting the one possible gap on the off side and he gloriously drove the ball, which thundered all the way to the boundary. Botham had kept his nerve and was the hero as England won by three wickets. Botham won awards for best bowler and fielder of the match, but Javed Miandad won the main award for his inspired batting display.

The match, which had featured the one-day debut of Mike Gatting, was also umpired by one Shakoor Rana. Ten years later in 1987, during a Test match in Faisalabad, they were both involved in a controversial incident. Rana had accused Gatting of changing the placement of the field as bowler Eddie Hemmings came in to bowl. It led to much finger wagging by both and they were also accused of using foul language. The incident led to the game being stopped only to be resumed the following day. England had already been upset because Rana had worn a Pakistan sweater during the Test and also Mudassar Nazar's cap. Rana said he would not continue to umpire in the Test until he received an apology from Gatting. With the threat of losing the England captaincy, Gatting finally delivered the requested apology to Rana.

Friday, 23 December had also seen Geoff Boycott, John Lever and Geoff Cope play in a local club match while the rest of the team were in Sahiwal. The game saw Boycott making a hundred. Lever damaged his back when fielding and Cope's day, uplifted by the news that he had become a father six weeks early, was somewhat let down by the wicket-keeper's inability to stump anyone off him.

On Christmas Eve, Geoff Boycott then found ten other members of the team to play with him at the charming Gymkhana Ground and made his usual hundred, but Boycott apart, only Mike Gatting, Bob Taylor and Derek Randall batted!

Christmas Day and the indefatigable Boycott was prepared for more practice, but the rain set in and exercise over the next few days was restricted to running, golf and squash! Meanwhile the president of the Pakistan Board of Control, Chaudry Mohammad Hussain, stated that fast bowler Sarfraz Nawaz had betrayed his country over his dispute regarding match fees and expenses and would not be considered for selection for the remaining two Tests. Hussain was due to meet up at the airport with the International Cricket Council's chairman David Clark and secretary Jack Bailey to discuss the first round of talks regarding matters relating to Packer World Series Cricket.

However, the talks were postponed until the next day because of a flight delay. The next couple of weeks would see further talks taking place in Bangalore, Melbourne, Christchurch and Port-of-Spain.

England, after celebrating Christmas in Lahore, were back at the Gaddafi Stadium on Boxing Day to face the Habib Bank XI in a three-day match, however, the rain put an end to any possibility of play commencing. The match should have started on the Monday, but saw no play on the Tuesday either and both teams then agreed that they would be better off playing a newly arranged one-day thirty-over match on the Wednesday instead, with the overs consisting of eight balls. The three-day match, therefore, was abandoned. It was hard even for the locals to ever recall a match where no play had been possible in the history of first-class cricket in Lahore. After even a little rain, the clay soil becomes sticky, and in mid-winter even in Pakistan there is not much sun to dry it out.

Some of England's bowlers had had little or no match practice over the past week and a half and needed the exercise more than the batsmen. After the match against the Habib Bank XI, there would only be the second one-day international before the second Test in Hyderabad. Chris Old had to miss out, although his injured knee was responding well to treatment, whilst John Lever played, having only just recovered from injuring his back in the club match just before Christmas.

The Habib Bank XI included, at the request of the selectors, a couple of outsiders, but they were still arguably the strongest first-class side in Pakistan. On a pitch that would not normally have seen play commence, the Habib Bank XI's captain, Javed Miandad, was in a quandary as to what to do when he won the toss. Would Miandad choose to see his players flounder on a slippery surface or face Bob Willis on a pitch with damp patches? He chose to field.

Opener Geoff Boycott, methodically going about his business, nearly batted through the innings, but in the 28th over he was bowled by Jamshed Hussain for 56. Derek Randall, with

49, showed improvement. Brearley had already fallen lbw to Hussain for 11 and, with the score on 32, Brian Rose advanced to a ball which turned away wide outside the leg stump and was stumped for 3. Boycott and Randall then put on 73 for the third wicket.

An amusing part of England's innings saw Boycott taking exception to the line of left-arm spinner Abdul Raquib, who, finding the ball turned a lot from a spot well outside the off stump, hardly bowled anywhere near the wicket. In response to the line bowled by Raquib, Boycott then adopted a left-hand stance. The ball from Raquib was bowled closer to the wicket and, when delivered, Boycott reverted back when it was in mid-flight and played it for a single on the off side. Next ball Randall, favouring a back-handed sweep, hit the ball through the slips for four! England finished on 166 for 7 after their 30 overs.

Bob Willis opened the bowling and removed Talat Ali with his second ball. Not long after Ian Botham, moving the ball in the air, had the Habib Bank skipper, Miandad, caught in the gully by Graham Roope whilst driving at an outswinger. Wicketless spinner Phil Edmonds bowled well enough to bring himself to the forefront of the selectors' minds, as the Hyderabad pitch was one that favoured spin. Mansoor Akhtar, the batsman who shared in a world record opening stand of 561 with Waheed Mirza for Karachi Whites against Quetta in Karachi the previous winter, was run out by John Lever when on 13. It was an uphill task for the hosts and they fell well short, ending on 103 for 7 at the close. Arshad Pervez top scored with 31, before being bowled by Geoff Cope. Willis finished with 2 for 17 and Botham 2 for 7. England won by 63 runs and had yet to lose on the tour.

3

The Hyderabad Test and the Sialkot one-day international

Meanwhile at the ground a new pavilion had been built, but the dressing rooms were cramped. Geoff Boycott expressed a desire for his own room, so he got it. The toilet!

ENGLAND had a day between the one-day tour match against the Habib Bank XI and the second one-day international, which was to take place at the Jinnah Stadium in Sialkot. The ground had seen only one previous one-day international, when New Zealand had defeated the hosts in December 1976 by one run. England's only previous visit to the ground was when, as the MCC, they had drawn a three-day tour match against a Punjab XI, in which the current Pakistan batting coach, Nazar Mohammad, and father of the Test player Mudassar Nazar, had hit 140.

England travelled the near-80-mile journey from Lahore north to Sialkot, a city in the north-east of the Punjab province, at the foothills of the snow-covered peaks of the Kashmir. Sialkot was the birthplace and home of one of Pakistan's Packer rebels, Zaheer Abbas; in addition the cricket ground was one of the oldest in Pakistan.

For the second one-day international, Geoff Boycott took over the reins of captaincy. Mike Brearley had decided it was time for a rest, so the match proved to be the first time the Yorkshire skipper had captained his country. Boycott decided that he would go in at number six to give Graham Roope, Geoff Miller and Mike Gatting some time in the middle.

Meanwhile, with the second Test in Hyderabad starting on the Monday, Brearley, along with bowlers Bob Willis, Chris Old and Mike Hendrick, took part in a game for the local Gymkhana Club in Lahore. It was a case of proving match fitness for Old, suffering from an injured right knee and Hendrick, who was recovering from flu. Brearley had also decided to impose an 11pm entertainment curfew on New Year's Night for the whole squad as he wanted them all in the right mindset for the Test.

The crowd packed into the tiny Jinnah Stadium in Sialkot, surrounded by paddy fields and ringed by the snow-capped mountains of the Kashmir for the second one-day international. Some were even hanging on to railway signals at the railway end of the ground to catch a glimpse of the action and their heroes. Acting skipper Boycott won the toss and put Pakistan in. The hosts lost wickets at regular intervals and struggled against the pace attack of John Lever and Ian Botham. Apart from those two, England's other bowlers used were Geoff Cope, Geoff Miller, Phil Edmonds and Mike Gatting! Except for Mudassar Nazar's 33, the top order failed miserably. Nazar was out off the bowling of Cope, brilliantly caught by Derek Randall diving at mid-wicket. At 76 for 6 they looked doomed, but if it wasn't for a spirited seventh-wicket stand of 64 by the left-handers Wasim Raja and Hasan Jamil, it would have been a lot worse. Raja, who had been rumoured to be signing for Glamorgan, hit two huge sixes off Geoff Miller in his score of 43. There was a five-minute hold-up when he hit his second six, as quite a few spectators ran on to the pitch to offer him personal gifts and congratulations. Miller's over went for 18. Raja was finally bowled by Botham. Jamil fell for 28, caught behind by Taylor off Lever, who had inflicted most of the damage taking 3 for 18 and was eventually named bowler of the match. Spinners Geoff Cope and Phil Edmonds also bowled well and the latter was ill-rewarded with only two wickets from an impressive spell. Pakistan had been bowled out for 151 off 33.7 overs.

The plan to give the batsmen much needed practice was only partly successful. Brian Rose, although hitting 45, had yet to show his genuine class. His timing was poor and his bat not always straight in the drive. He was bowled by a faster ball by Iqbal Qasim with the score on 104, but even though Rose had struggled, he had contributed significantly to England's total. England had already lost Graham Roope, when the ball stopped on him off the bowling of Sikander and he was easily caught in the covers by Rashid for 7, and was soon followed by Geoff Miller, another Qasim victim for 16. Test reserve Mike Gatting was questionably run out for 5 and England were 112 for 4. Derek Randall, however, went on to complete a forceful half-century although he failed to get the match batting prize, but was compensated by the fielding one. Randall finished on 51 not out as Botham, for the second one-day international in a row, hit the winning runs with 17 balls to spare to see the tourists home. England had won the game by six wickets and with it, the one-day series, with one game still to play. Pakistan's Wasim Raja was named batsman of the match.

The match ended a hugely successful international year for the tourists with the only real setback being the loss of the Centenary Test in Melbourne back in March. They had yet to lose on the tour of Pakistan and all heads had now turned to Hyderabad and the second Test. The main talking point was whether Chris Old's knee injury would recover in time and if not, who would replace him? Would it be left-arm spinner Phil

Edmonds or all-rounder Ian Botham? They were both likely candidates, or would the selectors go for three spinners instead?

The tourists headed south and flew to Karachi on the coast of the Arabian Sea which was followed by a three-hour drive north across the desert on New Year's Day to Hyderabad.

It was predicted as the England players rolled up for practice on the afternoon of New Year's Day that the pitch would be devoid of grass. When England last visited five years previously the pitch did not look capable of producing a result and even on the last day the ball was not turning any more awkwardly than it did on the first day. The reputation of the pitch leading up to the Test was that it still took slow predictable spin so it was presumed the selectors would go for three spinners. Five years before, 'Deadly' Derek Underwood had produced match figures of 48-15-119-0. A finished match in Hyderabad was treated as a rarity. The only small hope of a finish was that the mud at Hyderabad was sometimes not as impeccably flat as that on other Test grounds such as Lahore or Karachi.

Chris Old though, who had appeared in a club match for the Gymkhana Club, had some reaction to his troubled knee. Meanwhile, as England prepared for the Second Test, they were heartened by the news that skipper Mike Brearley had been included in the Queen's New Year's honours list and had been awarded an OBE.

All hoped that the Test would be a riot-free affair after the disturbances that had taken place in Lahore during the first. Passions though were at an all-time high in a troubled country caused by political unrest. Even the last match, the second one-day international in Sialkot, had seen a police sergeant adopt a threatening attitude to a youngster straying over the boundary.

The crowd rose in indignation, promising to throw more than the customary orange peel. However, it needed a flamboyant show of conciliation by an officer and his dismissal from the scene of the sergeant to restore goodwill. He was then applauded which all agreed must have been a record for a police officer in these parts.

Hyderabad is the fourth largest city in Pakistan and the second biggest behind Karachi, in the Sindh province, with the River Indus running nearby on the outskirts. The ground where the second Test was to be played was the Niaz Stadium, named after Niaz Ahmed, the sports-loving commoner of the city who was the motivating benefactor of the building of the ground. The inaugural first-class match to be played on the ground was on 16 March 1962 when South Zone took on the Pakistan Education Board. The first Test that took place was England's drawn game in 1973, which also began on 16 March, in which Dennis Amiss had hit 158. Incidentally, the first ever one-day international hat-trick in the history of the game was recorded at the ground in 1982 when Pakistan's Jalal-ud-Din removed Australia's Rodney Marsh, Bruce Yardley and Geoff Lawson.

Wasim Bari won the toss and elected for the hosts to bat first. The day was to belong to Haroon Rashid, the Pakistan number four batsman, who hit 108 which included ten fours and six sixes! The 24-year-old bank employee had come to the crease with Pakistan at 40 for 2 after losing Sadiq, well caught by Bob Taylor for 9, and Shafiq for 13. Mudassar Nazar was up to his old tricks again, trudging along snail-like, and it took him two minutes short of three hours to record his 27, before he was caught by Phil Edmonds off spinner Geoff Cope.

Rashid and Miandad then put on 112 for the fourth wicket. Rashid was in scintillating form and in slamming six sixes recorded the most by a Pakistan batsman in a Test innings, beating Intikhab Alam's four against England on the same ground in the 1972/73 series. Each of them seemed to go higher and higher towards the clear blue sky and disappear further over the boundary ropes. He reached his fifty by thumping Cope over mid-wicket with a six and his century with another huge drive over long on off Geoff Miller. His fifty was reached after seventy minutes, his hundred in ten minutes short of three hours. Rashid's partner, Miandad, could not keep up! Miandad also hit ten boundaries (seven fours and three sixes), but was then pegged back by Lever and Edmonds and took forty-one minutes to hit his last eight runs. He ended the day 48 not out. Rashid finally fell, caught with a low return catch off his own bowling by Edmonds, for 108, and Pakistan had now reached 213 for 4. Wasim Raja was out without addition to the score with Brearley taking a straightforward catch at slip to give Edmonds his third wicket of the day, finishing with figures of 3 for 69. England would be looking forward to taking the new ball early in the morning, Pakistan finishing the day on 220 for 5.

The day would also see the chief martial law administrator General Zia-ul-Haq, call for a conference 'to take out the bad blood and rid the game of politics'. It was thought he would impose a total ban on the Pakistan Packer players. It was also assumed that he would have a meeting with ex-vice captain Sarfraz Nawaz, who was still in dispute with the board and who had been dropped for the current Test in Hyderabad.

On a sun-baked day two, from the start the new ball did the trick with Abdul Qadir out in the second over caught by Brearley at slip off Geoff Cope's spin. Wickets were then soon to fall in three successive overs. Wasim Bari was run out by Graham Roope with a throw from gully for 10, Iqbal Qasim then went, caught by Roope at second slip off Bob Willis for a duck and Liaqat Ali presented Phil Edmonds with a simple catch at short leg off John Lever, also out for nought. Pakistan had collapsed to 249 for 9. Enter Javed Miandad, who then went about the bowling hitting 40 precious runs, hitting Lever for a sizzling six over long on and cracking Bob Willis for two boundaries. He was left stranded, on 88, as Sikander Bakht had a complete misunderstanding with him and was left in no man's land, halfway down the wicket. Pakistan had been dismissed for 275. Edmonds finished with 3 for 75 and had maintained his excellent progress having worked on both his action and mental approach.

England began their reply and after just over an hour skipper Brearley went with the score on 40. When on 17 he flashed at a quicker ball from Iqbal Qasim and Wasim Bari took the catch. Geoff Boycott though was answering England's need for runs and he produced an innings of technical purity, unwavering concentration and tactical awareness. He was equal to the speed of Liaqat Ali, adopting a two-eyed stance to counter the left-arm slant, and handled the pencil-thin Sikandar Bakht comfortably. Even left-arm spinner Iqbal Qasim bowling to the rough end could not tempt him into making a false stroke. At the close of play, Boycott remained unbeaten on 71 in an innings lasting four hours that included eight fours. Unfortunately for the visitors, Brian Rose fell to the last ball of the day for 27, bowled by a fizzing leg-break from Abdul Qadir, which lifted sharply off the roughed-up end of the pitch. England closed on 123 for 2, still 152 runs behind.

The morning session on day three, in Hyderabad, turned into a nightmare for England and in just over one hour they collapsed from 123 for 2 to 191 all out due mainly to the fine leg-spin bowling of the youngster Abdul Qadir. This gave Pakistan a first-innings lead of 84. England lost seven wickets for 20 runs, four of them to Qadir in 16 balls.

It could be reasoned that the late-order batting collapse was due to the lack of match practice combined with facing an in-form bowler in a very favourable environment.

Qadir could turn the leg break much more than the googly and his high arm action could extract maximum bounce from most pitches he bowled on. His supple flowing action and high arm delivery made him a handful, and especially in conditions like these. He had started on the second day with a solitary over from the end Bob Willis's footmarks had made and, with the last ball of that first over, bowled Brian Rose from round the wicket.

Randall joined Boycott at the crease for the beginning of the day's play and, for a short while, they both looked comfortable, then the collapse began with the run-out of Boycott, Derek Randall holding his hand up in blame. Boycott had only added eight to his overnight score when he played Iqbal Qasim past backward short leg to Liaqat Ali, fielding 30 yards away. As he set off, and with Randall also having taken a few strides, the ball had gone to Liaqat quicker than expected, Randall called Boycott back but it was too late, the ball thundered into wicket-keeper Wasim Bari's hands and Boycott was run out for 79. Two runs and twenty minutes later Randall was also back in the pavilion. The batsman had mishit a low ball back to Qadir, who dived forward and took a good catch near to the ground. In his next over Qadir claimed the wicket of Graham Roope, also caught and bowled, when he drove loosely at the spinner. New batsman Bob Taylor faced only one ball, as he received a perfect leg-break from Qadir, which turned from the edge of the rough to hit the top of the off stump. England had now crumbled to 142 for 6. Phil Edmonds and Geoff Miller both soon departed, caught behind off the spinners, before John Lever attempted to defend his wicket in a similar fashion that had proved so successful in India the previous winter. Qadir though soon reverted to bowling over the wicket and broke through, bowling a googly to Lever and England were now 157 for 9. As is usually the case when everyone else struggles, the tail-enders somehow conjure up something to question the other batsmen's attempted scoring exploits! Bob Willis and Geoff Cope put on 34 for the last wicket in seventy minutes. It was thirty-five minutes after lunch when Cope was caught at backward short leg by Sadiq off another leg-spinner, Wasim Raja, for 22.

Abdul Qadir walked off the pitch with figures of 6 for 44, a record against England (just beating Fazal Mahmood's 6 for 46 at The Oval in 1954).

Not a lot happened for the rest of the day until the last over when Sadiq, on 22, was out pushing forward to Cope and Edmonds took the catch right handed at short leg off bat and pad. Pakistan had reached 55 for 1 at the close, a lead of 139.

England spent the rest day planning on how to save the second Test. A lot would depend in the second innings on the performance of opener and vice captain Geoff Boycott. There had been talk of differences building up between Boycott and other members of the team over the past couple of weeks around Boycott's mania for occupying the crease at times when it would clearly benefit the side more if he got out. The most obvious example was on Christmas Eve when he batted throughout a practice match at Lahore Gymkhana. Several England players were furious that day, feeling Boycott was guilty of a gross piece of selfishness. A reconciliation of paramount importance was now required as Boycott, one of the few to be able to master the spin of Abdul Qadir, was now needed to lecture his team-mates on the correct technique, and they had to be prepared to listen. Boycott's method against Qadir was basically simple. Either he goes right forward to smother the spin or he goes right back, giving himself as much time as is possible to see the ball off the pitch. The collapse on the third day was the result of a succession of indecisive shots when batsmen were neither playing fully forward nor positively off the back foot.

There were also thoughts on when Wasim Bari, the Pakistan captain, would declare. It would be a vital decision in picking the right moment. He had erred on the side of caution in the first Test when he allowed Pakistan's first innings to drag on into the third day and he could not afford to make a similar error this time round.

Mike Gatting, who was not playing in the second Test in Hyderabad, once again helped out the BBC radio team with some commentary. The facilities that the touring party stayed in were horrendous. Gatting stated that the team had been housed in a blue-painted hotel in the middle of the Sind Desert. The room Gatting shared with Graham Roope was extremely basic. The shower contained no hot water, so that was fetched from a tap. There was no bath, the carpets were bare, the mosquito net was broken, whilst the toilet was something that resembled a shower with some buckets! When the drains blocked up, the players had to paddle through three inches of water just to clean their teeth. It was not surprising that back trouble, insect bites and diarrhoea reigned supreme and if the players went out the back of the hotel they would be faced with a swamp.

Meanwhile at the ground, a new pavilion had been built, but the dressing rooms were cramped. Geoff Boycott expressed a desire for his own room, so he got it. The toilet!

General Zia-ul-Haq, Pakistan's military ruler, approved a pay rise for his country's Test cricketers after a meeting with the Board of Control. The Pakistan players would now receive £386 for a Test, instead of £276. There was hope as well that Sarfraz Nawaz, Pakistan's vice captain, who was in dispute with the Board and had returned to London, would be 'pardoned' and be available for the third Test starting in Lahore on 18 January.

On such a crucial fourth day of the Test for Pakistan most were baffled on seeing the hosts simply bat leisurely throughout the day with Wasim Bari only deciding to declare twenty minutes before the end of play. By that point they were on 259 for 4, setting England 344 to win.

The morning session saw Pakistan only score 65 in two hours off 23-eight ball overs and a winning position looked like it had been thrown away. Expectations were high for a sharp acceleration in the run rate after lunch with Haroon Rashid and Javed Miandad at the crease, unfortunately for Pakistan though, Rashid pulled a muscle.

This resulted in pantomime time between both the batsmen and captains. The 12th man raced on to the pitch with a pair of batting gloves telling him he should have a runner. An over later Rashid asked Brearley if he could use opener Mudassar Nazar. England skipper Mike Brearley then objected as Nazar, having batted already scoring 66, would have known the fielders too well and also was a faster runner in between the wickets. Rashid then requested Wasim Raja, but now it was the turn of Miandad to object. Pakistan captain Wasim Bari came out for further discussions and finally it was agreed, surprisingly by all, that he would be acceptable. When he had finally arrived at the wicket reporting for duty there was then confusion about how they should go about using the runner. John Lever was bowling over the wicket and the non-striker was widely separated from the runner at square leg. After one over and one hazardous run they decided it was all too difficult and gave up.

Rashid, handicapped by the pulled muscle, limped between the wickets whilst the fleet-footed Miandad batted at the other end. Their stand of 71 in 110 minutes ended when Rashid mishit spinner Cope to Brearley at square leg. Miandad was joined by Shafiq, but did not really get to grips with the tight bowling and the defensively set field. When Bari declared with the total on 259 for 4, Miandad was 61 not out. The wickets had been shared two apiece by Geoff Cope and Bob Willis. The scene in place that fourth day had been that of Bob Willis charging in to bowl to the sound of wailing from the minarets and the mosques with the carrion birds floating around up above in the terrific heat.

Play was held up for five minutes while the police chased and caught a spectator. When the crowd demonstrated and got restless, he was released and carried off shoulder high by other spectators! This all added to help delay England's innings. The interval between innings had been stretched to fourteen minutes and Brearley and Boycott safely negotiated two overs before the close. England would now have to bat through five and a half hours' play on the final day to earn a draw that seemed highly improbable at the start of the day's play. The Pakistanis' tactics on day four had been a mystery, much to the infinite relief of England who were aware of the need to bat at the top of their capability.

The anxious fifth day for England began with openers Boycott and Brearley calmly batting through the first hour, supporting the views of many that the second innings was going to be easier than the first. Boycott had been dropped when on 23 and then again after eighty minutes of play at short leg by Sadiq off a Qadir googly, which seemed to turn and bounce more than most. Technically and temperamentally they were both superb and an hour after lunch they sailed into easier waters. The nearest that Brearley came to a mishap was when playing Qasim on the on side, he almost gave a return catch off the outside edge. There were several loud shouts for leg before, but the batsmen were staunchly supported by the umpires who did not give an lbw decision throughout the whole match. Thereafter, they were seldom in trouble as the match went on to a tragicomic end. The match should have ended after thirty minutes of the final hour, but at that point, Boycott was on 99 and Brearley claimed the extra half-hour to let him reach his 15th Test hundred. This took another quarter of an hour and, unfortunately when on 74, Brearley was caught at backward short leg off bat and pad by substitute fielder Hasan Jamal off the bowling of spinner Wasim Raja. England finished on 186 for 1, Boycott 100 not out.

England had to wait until mid-afternoon until the danger was well past, but until then there was always a fear that if a wicket fell, the new batsman would have had to grapple with problems which his predecessors had worked hard to solve.

With the pitch slower and with little bounce, Abdul Qadir tired and started pitching short, which he only did once in the first innings, and consequently was hooked for several fours by Boycott. There were no interruptions to the play on the final day until mid-afternoon, when small boys began coming on to the pitch, pursued by police with fleetness of foot, not usually a qualification associated with the police in these parts. Geoff Boycott had done the job expected of him and rightly picked up the man of the match award. The lengthy pre-match batting practice had paid dividends as Boycott and Brearley put on 185 for the first wicket, the highest opening partnership for England since Boycott and Dennis Amiss put on 209 at Port-of-Spain on the 1973/74 tour of the West Indies. Looking back on the game, Bob Willis stated that everything about the Hyderabad Test had been awful apart from Haroon Rashid's batting, going on to add that the Test had been fairly tedious, and that 'our' hotel was so poor that John Lever was sick as soon as he entered his room because it smelt so much.

England though had wriggled out, with some honour, of what had looked like a desperate position, and were now suitably relieved to finish the day heading over the desert to Karachi.

After a couple of days England travelled back north to Bahawalpur in the Punjab to play the district side in a three-day game. The city, the 12th largest in the country, was famous for its palaces and its nawabs (rulers). The match would be played in the Bahawal Stadium, known to the locals as the Dring Stadium, which could house 15,000.

The first day of the tour match at the Bahawal Stadium belonged to 24-year-old Mohsin Khan who batted five and a half hours for 97 not out. Khan was on the verge of winning his first Test cap and this weighed heavily at the start of his innings. Snicking the second ball of the match over the slips for a single, he then went ninety-three minutes without adding to his score. After his tense start he opened up a little, showing a pleasant range of shots and by the end of the day had hit 44 of his runs in boundaries.

Mike Brearley lost the toss for the fifth time in a row on the tour, but any regrets soon disappeared, as Chris Old and Mike Hendrick made splendid use of the new ball, reducing the hosts to 13 for 3 in the eighth over. Further wickets were taken by Ian Botham and Geoff Miller and resulted in the hosts going in at lunch on 77 for 5. Miller continued bowling impressively, taking two wickets in three balls in the afternoon and finishing the day with 4 for 52, whilst Old had figures of 2 for 23, a bowling display which would put him in contention for a recall to the Test team for the third and final Test. When Phil Edmonds removed Maazullah Khan before the end of play the Punjab XI had finished on 217 for 9, with the day belonging to Test hopeful Mohsin Khan.

The Punjab XI declared on their overnight score, leaving England to contend with a day of leisurely batting practice on the second day of this tour game. Brian Rose and Derek Randall both started the day in desperate need of runs and they would not disappoint, sharing an opening stand worth 137 and by the close, England had reached 242 for 2. Just like on the first day a large crowd packed into the picturesque ground. England were content to give the middle order batting practice ahead of the third Test, rather than try to score quick runs.

The day provided little entertainment with England going in at lunch on 63 without loss off 27 overs. The only adventurous shot before lunch occurred when Rose pulled Naeem Ahmed for six. Only when Rose and Randall reached their half-centuries did they have any inclination to accelerate the scoring rate. Rose finally fell to Wasim Raja's leg spin for 72, driving a simple catch to short extra cover. He had batted for three hours and twenty minutes, having hit seven fours and *that* six.

Randall was out straight after tea for 87, lbw to left-arm spinner Naeem Ahmed. Graham Roope and Geoff Miller batted until the close, with Roope 51 not out.

England had only themselves to blame for not winning on the third and final day of the tour match. They allowed their first innings to drag on for seven and a half hours in scoring 334 for 5 before declaring. Skipper Brearley was content to give his batsmen as much practice as possible. Graham Roope scored 85 before being run out.

This left the Punjab XI three and a half hours to survive as they trailed by 117 on first innings. They had reached 193 for 9 at the close, a lead of 76, with skipper Wasim Raja being the saviour with 49. Phil Edmonds was England's main wicket-taker with 3 for 50.

With three matches left on the Pakistan leg of the tour, England, after playing ten tour matches, had yet to lose, but had drawn six.

The events on day three of the tour match in the Punjab were overshadowed by the news that Pakistan had recalled two of their Packer players, opening batsman Zaheer Abbas and all-rounder Imran Khan, for the third Test in Karachi. This was hailed as a major breakthrough for Packer, which could help him to achieve a compromise between his World Series Cricket and the international authorities. With not only Pakistan, but also the West Indies keen to use their Packer players in official Tests, it certainly began putting pressure on England and Australia to do so as well.

However, the message from Lord's was loud and clear. 'What other countries choose to do is not our affair. We picked 17 for the tour of Pakistan and New Zealand and will not go outside those players.'

Australia would soon be choosing a tour party to visit the West Indies and Packer, as controversial as ever, stated that the Australian board would be risking contempt of court if they ignored his men for the tour party.

4

The Pakistan leg
of the winter tour
comes to an end

*The ball cracked into Brearley's ulna bone just
above the wrist and broke his left forearm.
Ironically, it was the only ball to behave
dangerously, and for the rest of the match it
tended to keep low.*

ENGLAND now had only three games left on their tour
of Pakistan: the third and final one-day international in
Lahore, followed by a one-day game against a Sind XI in
Karachi, and finally the big one, the deciding third Test, also
in Karachi.

England stayed in the Punjab and headed further north,
returning to the Gaddafi Stadium in Lahore for what was the
third and final one-day international, a series in which they had
already won and were leading two-nil. A surprise inclusion in
the Pakistan team for the one-day game was Sarfraz Nawaz,

who had apparently kissed and made up with the Pakistan Board of Control, presumably offering the apology which was a prerequisite of his return.

The Board had decided to increase Test fees by 2,000 rupees a Test and, by bizarre coincidence, not only was Sarfraz named in the one-day team, but Pakistan had called up Zaheer Abbas and Imran Khan for the third Test. The pair had been released by Packer, though the Pakistan Board of Control insisted they had not contacted the Australian TV tycoon because they did not recognise him or his organisation. Imtiaz Ahmed, chairman of selectors, only heard of the news when it was leaked on radio and in the newspapers. The Board, however, stated that they had never officially asked for the players to be released, but instructed the selectors that if they turned up in Karachi then they should be chosen. The scenario had become slightly baffling to all concerned, especially the Pakistan players and officials.

England, meanwhile, were preoccupied with the countdown to the final leg of their tour of Pakistan, but why should Packer make two of his squad available to Pakistan for an official Test after he had deliberately chosen dates that clashed with his own matches? England tour manager Ken Barrington was keeping silent on the issue, 'There is a lot I would like to say.'

England went in to the one-day match selecting from 13. Brian Rose was rested having played continuously of late and Bob Taylor asked to keep wicket so Paul Downton had to drop out. Geoff Miller decided he would rather bowl at length in the nets than be restricted to just seven match overs. Pakistan, meanwhile, dropped Sadiq Mohammad who was having a poor season.

Mike Brearley at last won the toss at the Gaddafi Stadium and inserted Pakistan. A grey cold morning of spitting rain had started with British Prime Minister Jim Callaghan and General Zia-ul-Haq, and their entourages, rushing up to the stadium in a noisy cavalcade, watch seventy minutes of play, shake hands with the players and rush off again!

Mohsin Khan, who had impressed a few days earlier for the Punjab XI, top scored once again, this time making 51 not out in a Pakistan total of 158 for 6 off their 35 overs. Pakistan's innings only included seven fours and one six, over half of them being scored by Khan. Mohsin confirmed the favourable impressions he had already made and played with a panache rivalling Miandad's and must have made a case for inclusion in the Pakistan team for the final Test. The ball turned from a spot just outside the off stump and moved a little off the pitch for the faster bowlers. Two wickets were claimed by John Lever and Phil Edmonds with one apiece for Chris Old and Geoff Cope. England conceded 46 runs in the last five overs.

The script was written for Sarfraz in this his comeback game and soon he had the wickets of both openers, Boycott and Brearley, in a fine opening spell. In fact, Sarfraz should have had a wicket with his first ball as Boycott steered into the hands of Shafiq at slip, but the ball bounced out again. In Sarfraz's second over, Brearley was caught at slip by Shafiq bat pad and then, in his third over, Sarfraz brought one back and got Boycott out, leg before. England were 15 for 2. Sarfraz was soon to have opening bowling figures reading three for 7 from five overs. Mike Gatting was caught in two minds by Hasan Jamil, the left-arm medium pacer, and then Ian Botham played two perfectly timed back-foot strokes on the off side, hinting at signs of a possible revival. Not long after, Botham was caught at the wicket by Wasim Bari as he aimed to steer Qasim towards third man. This was followed by Chris Old who was caught in the covers by Wasim Raja, whose fielding was athletic throughout. Now it was 49 for 5, but Graham Roope and Derek Randall immediately steadied things by scoring 48 in nine overs, but Randall fell for 32, to a splendid running catch by Mudassar Nazar at deep mid-wicket off Raja. Sarfraz still had three overs to bowl, but was not needed as Raja, named man of the match, mopped up the tail, to finish with 3 for 23. England were all out for 122 and had lost their first game on the tour by 36 runs. The consolation for England had been the winning of the one-day series 2-1.

The next tour match for England was a one-day game against the Sind XI made up of 35, eight-ball overs. England batted first at the National Stadium in Karachi, at the same ground that would be used for the final Test. Mike Brearley and Geoff Boycott, however, would be batting for the last time together on the tour. In the fifth over, Brearley faced Sikander Bakht who made a good length ball fly off the pitch. The ball cracked into Brearley's ulna bone, located just above the wrist, and broke his left forearm.

Ironically, it was the only ball to behave dangerously, and for the rest of the match it tended to keep low. Brearley retired hurt on 5. He said afterwards, 'The ball reared about head height and I suppose I was instinctively protecting my head. One of the several ironies was that it was England who asked for the bowlers to have unrestricted run-ups to give our quick men a workout. But, of course, we expected the pitch to be a lot flatter than it was.'

The bowler, Sikander Bakht, was compared to a stick insect, considered by some to be the skinniest man ever to have played Test cricket.

England's only spare batsman for the last Test was 20-year-old Mike Gatting, who had played only one first-class innings on the tour. Against the Sind XI, however, Gatting showed spirited skill with a top score of 59 and a stand of 86 in 12 overs with Ian Botham, who scored 47. England closed on 141 for 5 off their 35 overs.

Immediately following the Brearley injury, Geoff Boycott took over the captaincy and led the England team out for the Sind XI reply. Mohsin Khan, for a third match in a row, reached a half-century. It was Mohsin who steered the hosts towards victory with 59 before he was caught by substitute Graham Roope off Mike Hendrick. The bowlers, nevertheless, had a good workout, especially Bob Willis who finished with 4 for 17 off his seven overs. The Sind XI inflicted England's second defeat of the tour and second in a row, winning by three wickets with ten balls to spare. The game was overshadowed, however, by the injury to Brearley and he was taken to the Karachi hospital where his arm was set in plaster. Brearley prepared himself for the flight back to London for an operation in which physio Bernard Thomas believed he would have to have a pin or plate inserted.

As Geoff Boycott braced himself for his first Test as captain of his country he walked straight into a row between the cricket Establishment and Kerry Packer's circus. The England players declared their total opposition to any of Packer's Pakistanis playing against them in Karachi. Packer had freed three of them, Zaheer Abbas, Imran Khan and Mushtaq Mohammad, to play in the game.

Before departing for London with his broken arm in a sling, Mike Brearley had read out a dramatic statement. 'The English touring team are unanimously opposed in principle to players contracted to World Series Cricket being considered for selection for official International Cricket Conference Test matches.'

Manager Ken Barrington, meanwhile, added that the players' opinion was not just about the third Test, but also the West Indies' plan to include Packer players in their home series against Australia, stating, 'Our players think it is totally wrong that these players should be allowed to play and, in this instance, be flown from Australia and, at the end of the Test, return to the Packer series.' Barrington continued, 'Our team are not concerned about being beaten – that isn't the reason. They are concerned about the future of the game.'

How the three Packer players came to be recalled from Australia was still proving a mystery. The Pakistan Cricket Board (PCB) insisted that they did not summon them and that its last contact was before the present series. The PCB was then told to talk to Packer – but did not pursue the matter. However, the chairman of selectors said after the final one-day game that the players would be considered for the Test.

Rumours had begun circulating that a Pakistani journalist telephoned the Packer organisation in Sydney, and as a consequence the three players were released on condition they returned to Australia on 25 January. A lot of questions were being asked.

Just prior to the third Test in Karachi, Mike Brearley had arrived at Heathrow Airport in London to be met by chairman of England selectors Alec Bedser and was then quickly hurried away to see a doctor. 'The doctors in Pakistan say it will be at least three months before I am playing again,' said Brearley. He then commented about the Packer Pakistan affair. 'It is not up to Packer to decide who plays in the Test matches. The statement was to show the players' feelings. If you have been playing a very hard and arduous Test match, it seems wrong to me that your place could be taken by people released by Packer.'

Brearley ended up in a Birmingham hospital for an operation where a metal plate was inserted to support the bone fracture whilst it healed.

Karachi, the venue for the crucial final Test, is the largest city in the country and is the main seaport and financial centre of Pakistan. The National Stadium is the second biggest in Pakistan behind the Gaddafi Stadium in Lahore. Pakistan, before this Test, had never lost at the ground.

The day before the Test it all became apparent who the mystery contact was who had spoken to the Packer office in Sydney. He was Omer Kureshi, a former broadcaster who went to Singapore as an unofficial agent, not only to pick up the trio, but to meet Packer as well. Kureshi had no brief and was not recognised by the Pakistan Cricket Board, and it seemed strange that it was he who should undertake the negotiations. The question being asked was – since when was Pakistan's team being selected by agents outside their own selection committee?

Within hours of Brearley's injury, manager Barrington immediately requested cover and asked for Middlesex's Clive Radley to join the tourists in Karachi. Radley, who was coaching in Sydney, was expected to arrive in Karachi on the eve of the third Test. Along with John Whitehouse from Warwickshire, Radley had been paid £500 to remain fit in case he received such a telephone call and, following a benefit season with Middlesex, decided that winter he would stay fit by doing some coaching at Cranbrook, in Sydney, for Kerry Packer's World Series Cricket organisation. Initially when Radley received the letter he didn't give it much notice.

At 2am one morning Radley was awoken by his telephone. It was Donald Carr, the MCC secretary from Lord's, to inform him that he was wanted in Karachi to play in the third and final Test as Mike Brearley's replacement, and that he was booked on the 8am flight that morning out from Sydney. Radley quickly packed his cricket coffin and boarded the plane. However, the plane got into some slight fuelling difficulty en route and the captain had to land it in Bangkok, in Thailand, to refuel. The flight was delayed for longer than expected as an airline official informed Radley that, 'We can't get the undercarriage up.' Radley eventually arrived in Karachi on the morning of the Test and had to make his own way to the team hotel. On arriving and placing his luggage in his room he could not see any of the other team members anywhere, but heard voices coming from a room nearby. Skipper Geoffrey Boycott had the whole tour party in a room whilst on the phone to the authorities stating that England would not be playing in the game if Pakistan selected their Packer players. There was just an hour and a half before the start of play! The Pakistan authorities agreed and England headed for the National Stadium. Unfortunately though, because Radley had not arrived as scheduled the night before and had been travelling for 48 hours, England decided to pick Radley's Middlesex team-mate Mike Gatting. Radley's debut would have to wait!

Six months after returning from exile, 37-year-old Geoff Boycott would now become captain of England for the third Test and second phase of the tour to New Zealand.

'The last thing I wanted was to take over the captaincy this way,' he stated. However, Boycott's greatest ambition would now be fulfilled, having been denied it in the past by the appointments of Mike Denness and Tony Greig. It was thought to be one of the prime reasons why Boycott went into international exile in the first place.

Brian Rose, the Somerset opener, would now partner Boycott in the Test, but Brearley's absence would seriously reduce the strength of an indifferent batting line-up.

Geoff Boycott won the toss and had no hesitation in batting first. England had threatened not to play in the Test if Packer's Pakistanis were included and with that threat, England practically chose the team they would play against. Even without the three Packer players, Pakistan still ended having the better of the day.

With the score on 17, Brian Rose was brilliantly caught by Miandad at forward short leg off Sarfraz. Boycott and Derek Randall steadied things for just over an hour and a half before Boycott fell for 31, bowled by an Iqbal Qasim leg break that clipped his off stump. Boycott had been outwitted by a magnificent delivery. Derek Randall, having played two excellent hooks against speed, then found himself being Qasim's second victim in 11 balls; attempting to sweep on the front foot he was out lbw for 23. Enter young Mike Gatting and what a test this was to be for the 20-year-old, who had taken Mike Brearley's place and who also had kept emergency replacement Clive Radley out of the team. This was only his second first-class game of the tour and after one flowing off-drive off an Abdul Qadir full toss he was then completely deceived by a googly and was leg before for 5. Geoff Miller was then to receive a Wasim Raja googly that lifted viciously and Mudassar Nazar held the catch at short leg. England had now plunged to 107 for 5.

The spinners had done the damage, but the flow of wickets was halted by a resolute partnership of 45 by Graham Roope and Bob Taylor, which saw England close the day on 152 for 5. Roope had batted with increased authority and purpose, and using his feet nimbly to the spinners had made effective shots both sides of the wicket. England's much-needed recovery owed a lot, not only to Roope, but his able partner Bob Taylor, who batted intelligently.

Meanwhile, ex-England captain Tony Greig, now playing downunder in Packer's World Series Cricket, spoke about England's threat to boycott the Test if the Packer Pakistanis had been selected. 'I don't believe Brearley was behind the protest. It is far more likely to have been Boycott and he should be the last person to suggest who should play. He's never been around when needed.'

Roope and Taylor added another 37 to their partnership on the second morning before Roope fell lbw to Sikander Bakht for 56. The ball however pitched outside the leg stump and was drifting away, but Roope, who was playing a crucial innings, went across the wicket and tried to force the shot. Unbelievably umpire Amanullah's finger went up and England were 189 for 6. Bob Taylor went for 36, adjudged lbw to an Abdul Qadir top-spinner and then Phil Edmonds fell, leg before as well, to a googly which turned a considerable distance. Both shared doubt over their decisions. Six leg before decisions were finally recorded in the England innings and controversy reigned. This was only the second time in Test history that there had been as many as six leg befores given in an innings, England also being the victims of the previous record in South Africa in 1955. John Lever, with a spirited 33 not out, saw England finally reach 266 all out. It had been a nine and a half hour drudge full of ineptitude and boredom. The spinners, Iqbal Qasim, with his orthodox left-arm spin, Abdul Qadir, with a mixture of leg-breaks and googlies, supported by Wasim Raja, also bowling spin, had all bowled well. But it could be argued they had been allowed to. Eight of the ten wickets had fallen to spin, but England's batsmen were furious with some of the umpiring decisions that had been made.

Pakistan had 16 overs to face before the close of play and reached 54 for the loss of Shafiq Ahmed, who, taking a free swing off Bob Willis, was superbly caught by Ian Botham, temporarily substituting for Brian Rose. Botham hurled himself to a slightly fine position from square leg to take the catch. That brought 24-year-old Mohsin Khan to the crease on his debut, and he oozed confidence, magnificently striking spinner Geoff Cope for two successive boundaries to bring the fifty up in the 15th over.

40,000 excited fans packed into the stadium for the crucial third day's play, which could determine a major part in how this series would evolve. In quieter passages of play there were exchanges of dust bombs as the sun beat down on the sun-parched Karachi National Stadium.

In all, the crowd was well behaved apart from play being held up for ten minutes as John Lever was pelted with oranges and sundry debris whilst fielding at deep mid-wicket. Only one person, a child, rushed on to the pitch when Wasim Raja hit Geoff Cope for six. It was only at the close of play that the first serious invasion took place, as hundreds swarmed on to the pitch, scaling the ten-foot-high steel-reinforced barricades.

Pakistan had added 176 to their score, closing on 230 for 5 and so, after three days of the Test, were still 36 runs behind England. New wonder boy Mohsin Khan was the first wicket to fall on the third day when, on 44, he drove Cope straight and hard to Bob Willis at mid-off. England contained the Pakistan batsmen until Phil Edmonds then removed both Haroon Rashid and Mudassar Nazar in the space of four balls. The crowd were finally glad to see the back of the patient opener Nazar and when in his sixties they had began chanting 'Get out Mudassar'. On 76, he misjudged a length ball from Edmonds and lobbed the ball to substitute Botham, at mid-on. Edmonds turned into England's hero of the day as, with the last ball of play, Javed Miandad fell to his orthodox turn from leg, to give a slip catch to Graham Roope. Edmonds finished the day with figures of 3 for 44 off 22 overs.

Thoughts would now turn to day four after the rest day, and what the Pakistan spinners might conjure up, especially after witnessing the exploits of Edmonds. It would be a struggle for England as the batting was frail. Would England be getting anything out of the game apart from the commemorative gold medals – worth £50 each – presented to them by General Zia-ul-Haq?

After the day's play England captain Geoff Boycott headed straight for the hotel that was being occupied by the General, who had invited Boycott round so they could chat about various things including the Packer situation.

Boycott said, 'It is true that he invited me round for tea after the end of play and I went straight round from the ground. The General was not there for he had some urgent business to attend to, and when he came he apologised for being late. Yes, we had a very nice tea and I was with him for half an hour, but that is all I am prepared to say about the meeting.'

England now only had two days left of the tour in Pakistan and had to be fully switched on so that no last-minute disasters would see them leave disappointed. They had been expected to comfortably draw the Test and the series, in which the inexperienced Pakistan, without doubt, had provided the most memorable moments. On a pitch getting slower and slower they were expected to bat for at least six hours to grind out a draw and should not get complacent. The squad were longing for the next leg of the tour to New Zealand and what it offered in the way of luxuries, food and comforts. The bowlers could also look forward to the pitches, juicy and green. England's seam attack would then once again appear to be the best in the world. It would also provide the chance to see some positive cricket, but a good performance in New Zealand would not blind the true state of the England team, as seen in Pakistan.

Phil Edmonds continued on the fourth day just where he had left off at the end of the third. England's fielding was flawless apart from Edmonds having Abdul Qadir dropped at slip in his first over of the day. In 13 overs Edmonds took five wickets for 27 and Pakistan's innings, which had been swinging along busily, had crumbled from 230 for 4 to 281 all out. The dangerous Wasim Raja was caught by Mike Gatting running hard at deep mid-wicket for 47 to leave Pakistan 243 for 6. Graham Roope took a sharp catch at slip when Qadir drove in a cloud of dust. Two balls later Gatting, very close at point, picked up a low catch from Sarfraz. The unwell Geoff Cope bowled six overs before giving way to Geoff Miller, who had Wasim Bari leg before aiming at mid-wicket. When left-hander Qasim was bowled, swinging across a ball from Edmonds, the Pakistan innings ended on 281 with the hosts only 15 runs ahead. Edmonds had recorded the best ever bowling figures by an England player against Pakistan, taking 7 for 66.

Edmonds, the left-arm spinner, in the past had sometimes bowled too many loose balls to keep the batsmen under control. However, his line and length of late in the tour had been impeccable; he had now dropped into an excellent rhythm, and was thriving on his bowling. With Edmonds also being an excellent fielder, mainly standing at square short leg, he was expected to be a valuable member of the England set-up for a long time to come, certainly if his bowling remained as accurate and penetrative as his latest showing.

For the rest of the day England decided, well Boycott decided, to batten down the hatches. In the hour and forty minutes before tea he only produced one scoring stroke. He was there at the end after three and a half hours. Openers Boycott and Rose played the fast bowlers with the utmost safety except for one moment when Rose called for a single behind the bowler and was sent back. Miandad though, running round from mid-off, saw his throw go over the wicket-keeper's head. A ten-minute delay then occurred as the incident brought a shower of oranges on to the pitch! Much of the afternoon saw trouble on the terraces with the military eventually being sent in. None of it distracted Boycott, however.

The only wicket to fall was twenty minutes before tea when Rose, on 18, reached forward and was caught by Rashid at forward short leg off Qadir. After the interval Boycott leapt into action. He used his feet excellently against the spin of Qasim and ended the day 48 not out. Derek Randall at the other end was on 37 not out with England closing on 114 for 1, a lead of 99. Boycott had applied himself with painstaking care and had surely batted England to safety. The day, however, belonged to Phil Edmonds.

The final day started with Geoff Boycott seemingly set for another century, but on 56 he skimmed a drive and was caught by Miandad, hurling himself forward at cover point. Derek Randall thrashed two boundaries and, when attempting a third, saw himself bowled off stump by Sikander. It was great when these shots came off, but indescribably ugly when they didn't. A slow floating full toss greeted young Mike Gatting; like a child in a sweet shop he excitedly swung cross-batted and missed. Qasim had got him lbw for 6. Inexperience had got the better of him. Graham Roope struggled, not for the first time on the tour and once again Geoff Miller failed, out caught by Wasim Bari pushing forward to Qasim.

The final period of the Test began with Pakistan completing just nine overs in the first hour and with England scoring just 20 in seventy-five minutes. The Test once again had resulted in another dreary draw.

England finished on 222 for 5 and the series finished tied with all three Tests drawn, with Phil Edmonds picking up the man of the match award for his 7 for 66. Ten Pakistan bowlers had bowled in the England second innings. As it is, in these parts, the day would not be complete without some disturbance. A section of students took on the police and while an attempt to pull down the ten-foot-high security fence was thwarted, some tin advertising hoardings were torn down and beaten with sticks for the next few hours. Finally, chairs were thrown into the players' enclosure. Such were the scenes at a Pakistan home Test match in 1978.

The third Test was the 11th draw in the 12 played by England in Pakistan. The first at Lahore in 1961/62 had been won by England by five wickets.

Greeted by him when they had arrived in Pakistan, and seen off by him when they left, the England team were particularly fortunate to have, as their liaison officer, Shafkat Rana of Pakistan International Airlines. He was a major reason for this leg of the England tour running smoothly. In four days' time England would be far removed from all of the disturbances and hostilities in Pakistan, playing their first game on the New Zealand leg of their winter tour in the peaceful surrounds of Eden Park in Auckland.

The players had found Pakistan an extremely difficult place to tour, with little to do and nowhere to go. No TV, substandard accommodation and food, with the players having seen too much of each other. The pitches had been awful, the cricket turgid with incidents off the field a lot more animated than those on it. Pakistan had been determined to avoid defeat at all costs, and did not do themselves justice.

England left Pakistan having drawn all three Test matches, but winning the one-day series by two games to one. All of the other seven tour matches had either been won by England or were drawn.

5

England arrive in New Zealand for the second leg of the winter tour

Willis jigged round the field celebrating for nearly a full minute and later said, 'The lads are calling me Houdini now'.

ENGLAND wasted no time in heading for the more comfortable surroundings of New Zealand, the land of the long white cloud. The second leg of the winter tour would consist of nine tour matches, including three Tests, in Wellington, Christchurch and Auckland. The tour would begin and end in Auckland and the itinerary would not include one-day internationals, with the only one-day game being against Northern Districts in Hamilton. The schedule would see England play three-day tour matches against Auckland, Central Districts, Canterbury, Otago and a Young New Zealand side. All the matches on the tour would consist of eight-ball overs, as had taken place in all of the games in Pakistan. Eight-ball overs were not replaced by six-ball overs until the beginning of the 1979/80 Australian and New Zealand seasons.

The abrupt transformation from the dust and frustration of Karachi had not been easy. Although both flights went without a hitch, and the connection between the two was made in less than twenty minutes with the help and efficiency of the Singapore Airport Authorities, the journey lasted twenty-one hours. The first sighting of the country was striking for the squad. From the plane they were immediately aware of the greenness of the land and its rolling undulating nature. It was a nice contrast for them after the arid brown of much of Pakistan where they had spent the previous nine weeks.

'When our plane landed in Wellington we all let out a mighty cheer!' recalled Bob Taylor as the touring party were glad to have finally reached New Zealand.

This, and the eight-hour time difference from Pakistan, hit most players and the practice in the build-up to the first tour match against Auckland at Eden Park was suitably gentle.

According to a number of players who had previously toured Pakistan, the latest trip was the most boring they had ever been on.

The cricket had been disappointing, the wickets lifeless, and the overall atmosphere very low-key. On arriving in New Zealand the players went on a great blow-out for the first few days in Auckland. The players had entered paradise and, after the deprivations of Pakistan, they could now drink milk again, eat salad and fresh meat, and savour treats like dozens upon dozens of oysters. Not surprisingly, they all found it quite easy to put on a bit of weight in those first few days. The players now realised that they were amongst people who liked to eat the same kind of foods as they did.

As the party arrived at their hotel in Auckland, they found out that only five hours earlier the building had had to be evacuated due to a fire! However, it was not long before the players settled down with captain Geoff Boycott stating that England, without their Packer players, Tony Greig, Derek

Underwood and Alan Knott, would find it hard to maintain their unbeaten record against New Zealand.

'Normally we would have the edge over New Zealand, but the Packer business has brought the sides closer. There were grave misgivings amongst Pakistan supporters about their chances against us without their Packer players, but the doubting Thomases received a sharp shock – the series turned out to be very close. I think the same will happen here.'

Manager Ken Barrington was hoping to give all the squad a run out before the first Test in Wellington on 10 February. He stated that during the Pakistan tour the England selectors had to concentrate on finding a Test line-up and give those players as much practice as possible. 'We have arrived here feeling that we have not had enough cricket.' He felt that some members of the party had been 'absolutely starved of cricket'.

England's first ever Test against New Zealand had been played in January 1930 at Lancaster Park in Christchurch, which England won by eight wickets. Maurice Allom starred with the ball for England, taking 5 for 38 and 3 for 17. The game in Christchurch had in fact been New Zealand's first ever Test match. In the 46 Tests played previous to this current tour in 1978, New Zealand had yet to win a Test against England.

That tour of New Zealand was an historic one in that it was the first time that a full England side had been there other than briefly at the end of a long tour to Australia. That first tour back in 1929/30, led by Harry Gilligan, was affectionately remembered as it had included the first Tests that New Zealand had ever played. But that series took place in the same winter that another England side played a series in the West Indies – neither side contained the best that the selectors could pick.

Normally a tour to New Zealand had been an anti-climax after an arduous tour of Australia, and had come at a time when most were longing for home. This tour, however, was eagerly looked forward to by the England side. They were in dire need of the attraction of new faces, more congenial diets and better cricket after the tour to Pakistan.

It had nearly been a full year since New Zealand had last played Test cricket, a two-match home series the previous February against Australia which they had lost 1-0. The first Test in Christchurch had been drawn after Australia had set New Zealand 350 to win. At the close the Kiwis were 293 for 8 with Bev Congdon 107 not out. They lost the second by ten wickets, at Eden Park in Auckland, Dennis Lillee the main destroyer, ending with match figures of 11 for 123.

New Zealand cricket was not exactly experiencing a golden era in its history when England visited. Their failures in other years against strong sides had usually been due to timidity. In 1966, and again in 1971, they cast away winning positions through being too shrewd and crafty. Under new captain Mark Burgess they now had a leader positive in outlook and one not afraid of winning. There was nothing wrong in his batting either as anyone who had witnessed his rousing 105 at Lord's in 1973 or his 104 at Eden Park in 1971 could see.

New Zealand had now played Test cricket for nearly fifty years and it was absurd to think that they had yet to defeat England in a Test match, especially having produced players of the calibre of Bert Sutcliffe, John Reid and Martin Donnelly. They had already beaten every other Test-playing country.

The tour would start at the famous Eden Park in Auckland and England looked forward to seeing some grass on the pitch! The square lay diagonally across the rugby ground and was amazingly unscarred from the continuous rugby that had been played including the British Lions' last Test of 1977. Auckland is the largest city on the North Island of New Zealand and lies in the very north. The pitch was not expected to be fast, but was well-grassed and it was thought that the faster bowlers, Old, Hendrick and Botham, would be able to move the ball about.

The Auckland team included the newly appointed New Zealand captain Mark Burgess, who, after semi-retirement, had let his golf handicap slip back to three. He had returned to Test cricket and at the age of 33 was back, full of enthusiasm. Burgess was now also available to lead New Zealand in England in the second half of the coming summer. However, Burgess was not captain of the Auckland team and in the match against England the honour went to Graham Vivian. Vivian, a left-handed bat, had won five Test caps for New Zealand; his first had been against India in Calcutta in 1965 which had also amazingly been his first-class debut. Vivian's last Test was to be in 1972, against the West Indies in Port-of-Spain.

Geoff Boycott's warning that his English batsmen might find trouble adjusting to the faster, grassier wickets in New Zealand after the dead ones in Pakistan was soon proved to be correct. England were dismissed on the first day by Auckland for a moderate total of 210.

Boycott himself was dropped at second slip in the third over before finally going on to make 32. Graham Roope and Ian Botham both scored 33 and jointly top scored. Their 44-run partnership was the best of the innings and at least made the score more respectable. The England batsmen struggled with their timing against John Cushen and 19-year-old student Martin Snedden, who took full advantage of overcast conditions after Graham Vivian had won the toss. Twenty-seven-year-old Cushen might have played himself into contention to be selected for the first Test. It was he who had Boycott dropped by Mark Burgess at slip, but finally got the scalp of the Yorkshireman two and a half hours later, this time Snedden taking the catch. After an hour England were on the defensive at 38 for 3. Cushen ended with 3 for 72 and youngster Snedden 3 for 35. There were two wickets apiece for Rochdale-born Warren Stott and John McIntyre with his slow left-arm orthodox spin.

England opening bowlers Chris Old and Mike Hendrick had twenty minutes before the close, but the visitors were heartened to see the ball beat opening batsmen Peter Webb and John Kasper several times. At the close, Auckland, in reply to England's 210, finished on 4 for 0.

Chris Old soon broke through in the opening session of day two and in successive overs he dismissed both the openers, Webb and Kasper. That brought New Zealand captain Mark Burgess to the crease and he did not disappoint in scoring an unbeaten 74, with Auckland declaring at the tea interval on 182 for 4, giving England a first-innings lead of 28.

The only excitement in the final session came when a man streaked naked across the Eden Park Oval to the delighted cheers of the apparently bored crowd. The incident held up play for five minutes and probably cost opening bat Geoff Boycott his wicket. Boycott, annoyed by the interruption, shortly afterwards pulled a good-length ball from fast bowler Martin Snedden, which was caught at mid-on by Warren Stott for 25. Brian Rose was 51 not out at the close and was showing no sign of repeating his previous cheap dismissal. His second innings to date had included one six and five fours with England finishing on 85 for 1, a lead of 113.

The final day of the three-day match saw the game end in a predictable draw, but it was enlivened by a fine century by Somerset opener Brian Rose. Rose had last scored a century eight weeks previously in Pakistan and his 107 was just the confidence booster that he needed. He was tentative early on, but as the innings developed, drove with great power, hitting one six and ten fours. Boycott declared when Rose was out, leg before, to seam bowler Warren Stott. The batting had been far superior to the first innings and the players obviously had become more used to the extra bounce of the wicket after the lifeless pitches in Pakistan.

England declared on 208 for 1 with Mike Gatting 43 not out, setting Auckland 237 to win in 200 minutes. They decided not to accept the challenge and by the close of play were 114 for 3 off 39 overs with opener John Kasper 61 not out. The match, therefore, ended in the expected draw. It had been a 'jet-lagged' game for the tourists.

Geoff Boycott decided to take a rest and dropped out of the next tour match, a 35-over game against Northern Districts, in Hamilton. The match was to be England's only one-day game of the tour. Paceman Chris Old and replacement batsman Clive

Radley would also miss the match because of injuries picked up during the opening tour match against Auckland.

Radley, flown to Pakistan to replace original tour captain Mike Brearley, had a badly bruised thumb, but an X-ray showed no fracture and he was expected to be in contention for a place in the first Test. Old, meanwhile, had a bruised shin and was unable to take the field on the third day of the Auckland game.

There were rumours about a plan to play on the rest day of the first Test if the match was affected by rain, but manager Ken Barrington was opposed to the plan. The New Zealanders were relying heavily on Test match revenue from the tour to pay their share of the costs arising from the Kerry Packer court case.

England headed the straightforward 125 kilometres south from Auckland to Hamilton's Seddon Park, a ground renowned for its 'village green' setting, which afforded a picnic atmosphere for spectators. The ground was named after former New Zealand Prime Minister Richard 'King Dick' Seddon.

Northern Districts, captained by John Parker, won the toss and put the tourists, led by Bob Willis in Boycott's absence, in to bat. It was his first match in charge of an English side. It was a disappointing batting performance with only Randall (24) and Botham (23) scoring more than 20 England reached 164 for 9 at the end of their 35 overs. Cliff Dickeson, a slow left-arm bowler, expensively took 3 for 58 whilst there were two wickets apiece for Richard Collinge, Brian Dunning and right-arm medium pacer Peter Anderson, who at 28 was making his first-class debut. He would only play six more first-class matches in his career after this game.

In reply, Northern Districts opener John Wright top scored with 27 before falling leg before to Geoff Cope. Wright was one of two new caps included in the side for the forthcoming first Test. With the score on 83 for 3 after 20.3 overs, at 5.08pm, the rain came and the umpires had no option but to abandon the game.

Local officials then decided that they would award the game to Northern Districts because they had scored their total in 20.3

overs, bettering England in their first 20.3 overs. Step forward England acting captain Bob Willis, who argued that England in fact had the better scoring rate. Willis correctly pointed out that under the playing conditions the England run rate should be calculated on their full 35 overs, instead of the first 20.3 when they were 56 for 3. England, therefore, ran out winners on a faster scoring rate.

'The last time I captained a side was at Sunday School,' Willis said. 'I spent all last night thinking about my field placings.' Willis had led his side from the front, dismissing opener Grant Gibson with the second ball of the innings.

Geoff Boycott, having been England's most successful batsman on the Pakistan leg of the winter tour, decided he would also drop out of the next tour match, a three-day encounter against Central Districts in New Plymouth, thereby giving the other batsmen a chance to strike form before the first Test in Wellington in a week's time.

'The batting is causing me more concern than any part of our game,' stated Boycott. His decision to drop out meant that Bob Willis would once again take charge. All of the specialist batsmen were chosen for the game, including Brian Rose, who had scored a century in the tour opener in Auckland. Boycott said that it was important for the Somerset batsman, who did not bat well in the Tests in Pakistan, to play against Central Districts to consolidate his form.

New Plymouth, named after Plymouth in Devon where its earliest settlers came from, is the major city in the Taranaki region on the west coast of the North Island.

Bob Willis won the toss for England and decided to bat and, for once, the tourists performed with the authority of an international side, with the two standout innings coming from Mike Gatting and Chris Old.

The ground at Pukekura Park in New Plymouth was one of the most picturesque match venues in New Zealand. The smallish amphitheatre possessed three sides with steeply terraced grass banks amid fir trees. The soil, between the snow-capped Mount Egmont and the sea, was volcanic and dry, and once the effect of the pre-match watering had diminished by lunch, the Central Districts spinners came into the match.

The fast bowlers began the day firing away and were played well by Brian Rose with customary application, and by Derek Randall until he was out; failing to pick up his bat high enough when deciding against a stroke, he was bowled off the under edge by Denis Aberhart for 17. Graham Roope bridged the transition between pace and spin and looked settled before a ball from David O'Sullivan turned sharply, hit his thumb and was caught by Robert Anderson at slip. O'Sullivan had played in Hampshire's championship-winning side of 1973.

Gatting, who had had few chances in Pakistan, batted with spirit and scored 66. His innings began battling pace and ended against spin and he scarcely made a mistake for two and a quarter hours. Gatting was confronted by two off-spinners, Doug Bracewell and O'Sullivan, and used his feet well, attacking with excellent judgement. When he lofted O'Sullivan into the covers, he was out to almost his only serious error.

Old, meanwhile, had hardly mustered a run on the tour to date so his 55 was most welcome to the tourists, ending the innings with a splendid piece of controlled hitting. Old made his first 54 in thirty-two minutes with nine fours, mostly perfectly timed through the covers, and two sixes, which were skimming pulls over mid-wicket. When Old fell, bowled by Alistair Jordan, Bob Willis declared with the England score on 296 for 6. Geoff Miller, who partnered both Gatting and Old, also batted well and had reached 31 not out.

This left fifty minutes for the Central Districts to bat until the close and both openers, Robert Anderson and Ian Rutherford, successfully held off Willis, John Lever and, for the last two overs Geoff Miller and Geoff Cope, to finish with the score on 29 for 0. Anderson was already included in the team for the first Test whilst 20-year-old Test prospect Rutherford had made 1,150 runs for Worcestershire's second XI two years previously.

The morning of day two saw Willis and Lever take four wickets in an admirable opening spell. Willis removed Anderson for 10, caught behind by Paul Downton, to a ball he hoped he would not get in the forthcoming opening Test. Central Districts also included in their line-up 'Jock' Edwards, a 22-year-old wicket-keeper who had hit a half-century against Australia the previous February. He came in to face the second ball of a Willis over and then proceeded to hit four off the remaining seven balls.

The ball soon began to turn, but the England spinners were handicapped by the umpires', Kinsella and Woodward, resolute refusal to give an lbw decision. With this knowledge the batsmen began to play with the spin, and an eighth-wicket partnership between Bracewell and O'Sullivan added 58. Paul Downton, England's wicket-keeper, playing in only his third tour match and only his tenth first-class game, scarcely made a mistake in the innings. As the Central Districts innings neared conclusion, Downton was seen to change direction and hold a brilliant left-handed catch, low down off an inside edge, to remove Denis Aberhart off the bowling of Chris Old for a duck. It was also encouraging to see Old fit and in form and ready to strengthen the Test team.

Central Districts had been dismissed for 198, Willis ending with 3 for 45 and off-spinner Geoff Miller with 3 for 56. There were two wickets apiece for Lever and Old, giving England a first-innings lead of 98.

Prior to England's second innings the mid-afternoon roller was applied, which resulted in the ball kicking off a good length and turning a lot on a dry pitch. This led to both the opening batsmen being hit, Clive Radley on the head and Brian Rose several times on the chest, after which there was a reluctance to suffer any further discomfort a week before the Test match. With England now having what seemed a winning lead, an innings of slog and self-preservation soon followed. England closed on 71 for 7, a score that sounded somewhat undignified, but with the state of the pitch, there were reasons for it. England finished day two leading by 169, with David O'Sullivan's bowling figures being 7.5-2-9-3.

It was up to 28-year-old skipper Bob Willis and spinner Geoff Cope to increase the lead, putting on 18 runs in a stubborn forty minute partnership on day three. Cope ended up top scorer with 20 in England's total of 104. Willis ended up scoring just one, however the time used up was to prove invaluable. Slow left-arm orthodox bowler O'Sullivan finished with excellent figures of 5 for 14, with England having set Central Districts 203 to win.

At tea, the Central Districts still needed 101 runs to win off the final 15 overs and the game was meandering into a draw. The final session, which had been shortened because of the tourists' travel plans, saw the hosts, however, make a bold bid for victory. With five overs left, 34 runs were still needed, at which point Willis brought himself and Chris Old back into the bowling attack. It did not take long for Terry Horne and Denis Aberhart to hit Old for 22 off two overs. Aberhart then hit Old into the covers, where Derek 'The Arkle' Randall sprinted 18 yards to take the catch. The match had now reached the final over with the last two batsmen, Horne and Jordan, at the crease. It was to be bowled by acting captain Bob Willis, with Central Districts still requiring five runs to win.

The first and fourth balls went for singles and then two runs came off the seventh, which brought the scores level. The fielders crowded round Horne, who was making his debut in first-class matches, to cut off the single, but Willis beat him with a ball that knocked out his leg stump. Willis jigged round the field celebrating for nearly a full minute and later said, 'The lads are calling me Houdini now.' The match had ended in a tie, the first time a first-class match had done so in New Zealand.

The nickname of 'Houdini' was apt for Willis, as it was he who had convinced the locals that England had won by a faster scoring rate in his first game in charge against Northern Districts in the previous tour game.

The tourists were enjoying any spare time they had to take in as much sightseeing as they could on the North Island. They

~ destroyed in 1886!

enjoyed a morning in Rotorua visiting the Green and Blue Lakes, and the Hot Springs, with the Pink and White Terraces fulfilling all the tourists' expectations of beautiful New Zealand and the mysterious Maori legends. The tour team then headed to the South Island.

England flew to the largest city on the South Island, Christchurch, for their game against Canterbury, the fourth of their New Zealand tour. The earliest known record of cricket being played on the ground was when, in January 1882, Alfred Shaw's visiting England XI played a Canterbury XVIII, in a two-innings, two-day match. The game ended in a draw, Shaw's team having bowled out the 18 men of Canterbury in their first innings for 100, with Billy Midwinter taking 9 for 29 and Tom Emmett 6 for 30.

Canterbury captain Bev Congdon won the toss and put the tourists in. It was not long, however, before England had a massive injury scare to skipper Geoff Boycott. Boycott's injury came in just the same way as Brearley's broken arm in Karachi, fending off a short ball. He was hit twice on the forearm by Dayle Hadlee and after the second blow retired hurt whilst on 9. Hadlee's brother, Richard, also opened the bowling and made the fullest use of the conditions, first getting opener Geoff Miller caught in the slips after a raft of streaky shots, followed by Clive Radley, lbw first ball. Ian Botham then played a careless shot and was bowled by Congdon without scoring. Radley had now notched up scores of 4, 28, 12, 11 and 0 and had done nothing to justify the confidence of the tour management to have him included in the party as Brearley's replacement. Gatting also failed, out for 5, but at least he must have known that he was ahead of Radley in the pecking order for the first Test selection.

At the fall of the seventh wicket and with the score on 156, Boycott returned, hitting only two more singles before he turned the dangerous Richard Hadlee off his toes to square leg and was caught by Stephen Boock. It was left to Chris Old, the England number eight, to bring about some respectability to the score. His lucky 51 saw England limp to a final total of 173 all out. Old gave one positive chance to slip when on 33, but he had innumerable near misses in between. He drove fiercely and hit five badly needed boundaries in his half-century.

Richard Hadlee finished with 5 for 50, brother Dayle 2 for 32 and left-arm spinner Stephen Boock 2 for 21. The bowling display would have given the New Zealand selectors massive heart and great optimism as they went about planning their attempt to win their first ever Test against England.

Canterbury made a mockery of the conditions as they raced to 26 for 0 off three overs by the close. Thirty-four-year-old Peter Coman hit Bob Willis for 14 runs off the last over of the day whilst the other Canterbury opener, Barry Hadlee, the eldest of the three Hadlee brothers playing in the game, was lucky to survive an lbw decision to Mike Hendrick.

A bizarre occurrence took place during the game when a man was walking across the ground as if out on a leisurely stroll. The man, apparently a sheep-shearer, had been coming home from an all-night celebration. When the waiting arms of the law greeted him, his explanation that he was in search of a pie was simply not good enough.

Canterbury had a relatively good morning on the second day and just before lunch were a trifle lucky to be 104 for 2. The ball did not move around as much as on the first day with Mike Hendrick unfortunate not to have more than the two wickets he had already claimed. After an hour and twenty minutes, and having bowled his best spell of the tour, the Derbyshire quick stuck out his left hand in an attempt to take a hard return catch. He collapsed in agony, with his little finger pointing in an unconventional direction. When the finger had been put back into place after it had been dislocated at the base, he was more than pleased to find that no break had occurred. The last eight wickets of the Canterbury innings then fell, for 40 runs, to Willis, Old and Botham and were down mainly to some excellent catching. Old, at first slip, and Willis held two catches each with Boycott gathering a good low one at mid-on.

The England squad assemble at Heathrow Airport, on 24 November 1977, before departing on what was to be a gruelling and punishing tour to Pakistan and New Zealand. (Central Press – Getty Images)

The official photograph of the England squad before the first Test, at the Gaddafi Stadium, Lahore, on 14 December 1977. (Author's Collection)

Back Row (L. to R.) :– M. W. GATTING. P. R. DOWNTON. G. MILLER. J. E. LEVER. B. C. ROSE. P. H. EDMONDS. I. T. BOTHAM.
G. R. J. ROOPE. G. A. COPE. D. W. RANDALL. G. G. A. SAULEZ
(Scorer)

Front Row (L. to R.) :– B. W. THOMAS. M. HENDRICK. R. W. TAYLOR. G. BOYCOTT. J. M. BREARLEY. R. G. D. WILLIS. C. M. OLD
(Assistant Manager)   (Vice-Captain) (Captain)
K. F. BARRINGTON.
(Manager)

ALLIED PHOTO Co.

Pakistan players Haroon Rashid, Javed Miandad and Wasim Raja, prior to the third Test at the National Stadium, in Karachi, on 18 January 1978. (Patrick Eagar – Getty Images)

England during a net session before the third Test at the National Stadium, in Karachi, on 18 January 1978. L to R; Brian Rose, Geoffrey Boycott, Paul Downton and Derek Randall. (Adrian Murrell / Allsport – Getty Images)

Captain Geoffrey Boycott batting, during the third Test in Karachi, January 1978. (Patrick Eagar – Getty Images)

Mike Gatting sweeps Iqbal Qasim, on his Test debut, the third Test in Karachi, January 1978. (Patrick Eagar – Getty Images)

Pakistan spinner Abdul Qadir bowling to England wicket-keeper Bob Taylor, as Graham Roope backs up, during the third Test in Karachi. (Patrick Eagar – Getty Images)

Wicket-keeper Bob Taylor and spinner Geoff Cope appeal, with Phil Edmonds looking on, as Pakistan's Mudassar Nazar survives an lbw appeal during the third Test in Karachi. (Patrick Eagar – Getty Images)

New Zealand win their first ever Test against England, as the tourists are dismissed for 64 at the Basin Reserve, Wellington. Geoff Howarth (arm in air, ball in hand) has just caught Bob Willis, off the bowling of Richard Hadlee. John Parker grabs a stump. (John Selkirk)

New Zealand's Richard Hadlee, holding stump and sweater, gets ready to lead his victorious team off the pitch, after taking ten wickets in the match. (John Selkirk)

Man of the Match, Richard Hadlee, leads the New Zealand team up the pavilion steps at the Basin Reserve, with captain, Mark Burgess, following. (John Selkirk)

New Zealand spinner Stephen Boock and England all-rounder Ian Botham chat in the Basin Reserve dressing room after New Zealand's historic Test win. (John Selkirk)

The Young New Zealand team line up at Temuka before their game against England. Standing, L to R: B. J. McKecknie, J. F. Reid, J. V. Coney, E. J. Gray, M. H. Toynbee. Seated, L to R: M. C. Snedden, D. W. Bracewell, G. N. Edwards, B. A. Edgar (captain), I. A. Rutherford, B. R. Blair, B. P. Bracewell. (From the New Zealand Cricket Museum collection)

Ian Botham celebrates his maiden Test century during the second Test against New Zealand at Lancaster Park, Christchurch. (John Selkirk)

Ian Botham's innings, having just completed his maiden Test century, comes to an end during the second Test against New Zealand at Lancaster Park, Christchurch. Botham is out for 103, caught by wicket-keeper Warren Lees off the bowling of spinner Stephen Boock. (John Selkirk)

Ken Barrington, the England manager, chats to Mike Brearley at Lancaster Park, in Christchurch, during the second Test. Brearley returned to New Zealand as a journalist after leaving the tour with a broken arm in Pakistan. (John Selkirk)

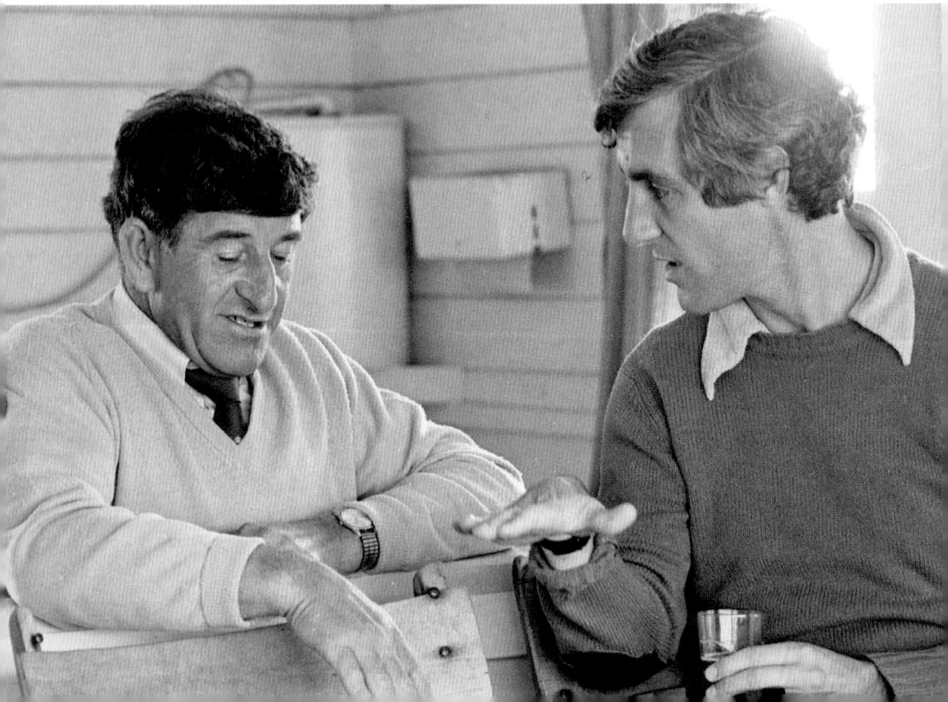

Canterbury had been bowled out for 144, giving the tourists a first-innings lead of 32. Willis ended with 4 for 46 with Ian Botham bowled well, taking 3 for 28.

After an early tea, England began their second innings, with Derek Randall and Geoff Miller at the crease. Regular opener Geoff Boycott's bruised arm had to be placed in a pressure bandage overnight. It was now less swollen, but still painful. It was the liveliest opening start to the tour, the openers making 45 in half an hour, greatly helped by Richard Hadlee's short-pitched bowling. Hadlee, who had looked pretty formidable in the first innings, was now well out with his deliveries and was hooked for 30 runs in three overs!

Randall was then dismissed for the second time in the match in the same way, leg before playing forward, this time to Boock for 23. Next over Geoff Miller went for 20, caught in the gully cutting at Bev Congdon.

Mike Gatting was pinned down for a while by left-arm spinner Boock, before deciding to charge him and was stumped by skipper Maurice Ryan for one. Three wickets had fallen for one run with England now 46 for 3. Clive Radley then concentrated hard for twenty-five minutes to avoid a pair, but when on 23, he pushed out to a Stead googly and was bowled. It was Botham who added spark to the England innings and ended the day with a flourish, finishing 58 not out, hitting the ball hard off both the front and back foot with strokes of quality. He batted vigorously and at least raised hopes that England's batting was not always going to be as bad as it had recently looked. Botham's 58 came off 89 balls in the last ninety-five minutes of the day. England closed the day on 135 for 4, a lead of 167.

The third day continued with Botham carrying on from where he had left off the previous evening with Bob Taylor now his active partner. The outfield on this large ground was not fast, but his strokes off the front and back foot were such that he hit 18 fours and a six. From 88, he raced to 104 made from 157 deliveries, by hitting Dayle Hadlee in five balls for a two,

two fours and a six. Botham's only error was when on 117 he brought about an extraordinary accident to the Canterbury opening batsman Peter Coman, offering a catch on the long-on boundary. The catch popped out of his hands and as he dived in an attempt to recover the ball, his jaw landed on it. He was carried from the field unconscious and did not come round for twenty minutes, which ended with him spending the night in hospital. Botham was on 126 not out and Taylor on 31 when Boycott declared England's innings on 230 for 4, leaving Canterbury a target of 260 to win.

Canterbury were soon reduced to 43 for 4 with Coman unable to bat and it looked like at that stage they would not survive the remaining 110 minutes, especially as Paul McEwan had already retired hurt after being hit on the head by Willis. It was down to two Test players, Bev Congdon and Richard Hadlee, to save the day for Canterbury. Congdon batted like a different man to that of the first innings, in which he was almost unrecognisable as the high scoring batsman of 1973 in England. He had hit 176 in the first Test at Trent Bridge and 175 in the second at Lord's. Congdon took root and Boycott, with his bowling reduced by the absence of Hendrick, decided against calling upon his fast bowlers for another effort. Hadlee rattled up 56, unusually batting better than he had bowled! Canterbury had reached 142 for 5 when the match ended in a draw with Congdon 32 not out. Both sets of Test selectors could take some encouragement from the drawn game.

The discussions between the New Zealand Cricket Board and the England management, regarding whether there would be play on the rest day of the Test if play had been affected by rain, was finally resolved. After a meeting, they decided that there would now be play on the day, but only if the second or third day's play was abandoned before 1pm. If the first two days were completely washed out, the match would become a four-day affair with play on the rest day. They also decided that the final Test of the three would become a six-day contest if the series was level after the first two Tests.

6

England historically sink at the Basin!

At this point Boycott stated, 'Now will people understand why I bat slowly!'

ENGLAND arrived for practice at the Basin Reserve in Wellington, two days before the first Test, to find the practice wickets still damp from the rain of two days earlier. The ground staff believed the pitches would not be needed until New Zealand's scheduled practice that afternoon.

The New Zealanders used the net wickets, while England's batsmen had to be content with a centre pitch workout, mainly involving spin bowlers. The groundsman looking after the Test wicket said he was not advised that the England cricketers intended to practice. 'I am very embarrassed about the whole affair,' he said.

England captain Geoff Boycott was disappointed with the mix-up because England's batsmen needed as much practice as possible if they were to adjust to New Zealand wickets after the lifeless ones encountered in Pakistan.

The eve of the Test saw the tourists include injured fast bowler Mike Hendrick in their team. Hendrick was still recovering from the dislocated little finger of the left hand that he had injured in the previous tour game against Canterbury, in Christchurch. Hendrick, along with John Lever, Bob Willis, Chris Old, Ian Botham and Geoff Miller, were the six specialist bowlers selected in the side. The unusually large number had been dictated by the poor form of England's batsmen during the tour.

The first Test was to be played at the picturesque Basin Reserve ground, where it was reported that the first ever game to take place was a match between the Mount Cook gaol prisoners and officers and the crew of HMS *Falcon*, which was docked in Wellington, in 1868.

The very first, first-class game to take place had been Wellington's match against Auckland in 1873, which was easily won by the home side, whilst the first ever Test match played at the ground was in 1930, the drawn second Test against England. It was a match in which the New Zealanders, after winning the toss, had seen their openers put on 276 for the first wicket, with Stewie Dempster hitting 136 and Jack Mills 117.

The morning of the Test saw Geoff Boycott win the toss and decide to put New Zealand in. Writing in the morning's *Christchurch Press,* Dick Brittenden stated that the pitch was not over-grassed but there was enough in it, with a very firm surface, to suggest that the seam bowlers would be in control for some time. There were bare patches at one end which could cause problems later on in the match, especially if they began to expand and crumble. Another factor to take into account at the Basin Reserve was that there was likely to be a wind of some strength.

England fast bowler Mike Hendrick, who had dislocated that little finger on his left hand, passed a fitness test an hour before the match started. It was Hendrick, along with Bob Willis, who wasted first use of the wicket by pitching the ball too short.

A big decision went the way of the home side right from the start. Willis was adamant that the first ball he bowled was nicked behind by opener John Wright. The umpire, however, was quick to turn down the bowler's appeal. A furious Willis, upset by the decision, then unleashed a barrage of bumpers which Wright and Robert Anderson easily weathered. The bowler in his fury twice sent balls flying over wicket-keeper Bob Taylor's head, giving away eight byes.

Chris Old finally got the breakthrough for England before lunch when, having conceded 21 runs in three overs, he also managed to claim the wicket of Anderson, caught behind for 28. Old bowled relentlessly during the afternoon session, bowling 18 overs unchanged, reducing New Zealand's run rate to a crawl. He also broke the dangerous 54-run second-wicket partnership of Wright and Geoff Howarth, when he had Howarth caught by Botham for 13, with the score on 96.

It had been a frustrating day for Old, who not only had several leg before appeals turned down, but also saw Wright dropped by Graham Roope at second slip off his bowling. The Yorkshire paceman certainly deserved a better return for his intelligent use of the conditions which were perfect for seam bowling. Boycott was let down though by his other quick bowlers, Willis and Hendrick.

The afternoon session was to see Willis, the England vice captain, back to his hostile best and, as the tea interval approached, he sent New Zealand captain Mark Burgess's stumps scattering all over the place with a ferocious delivery. Boycott was beginning to regret his decision to insert the Kiwis with his fast bowlers not getting the results that he was hoping for from the well-grassed wicket.

Opening bat John Wright was the main stumbling block throughout the day. The 23-year-old Derbyshire player, making his Test debut and having survived that confident appeal for a catch behind off the first ball from Willis, batted throughout the day for 55 not out. In fact, when Wright had reached his fifty it had taken him 272 minutes; only two minutes slower than Mudassar Nazar had scored during his record slow-scoring innings at Lahore in December. It had taken him 340 minutes to end the day on his 55. Bev Congdon finished the day on 26 not out with New Zealand on 152 for 3.

The gale of the previous night passed through, the clouds lifted from the surrounding hills, the sun shone and the bowlers at the beginning of day two had none of the struggle for control they had encountered on the previous day.

The Saturday's cricket had begun with the main stand vociferously all joining in to sing 'Happy Birthday' to Bev Congdon as he went out to resume his innings. The singing was led by a sprightly, 70-year-old lady from Palmerston North, who travelled the world watching cricket and was well known to all the diehard New Zealand cricket fans. Congdon was once asked how he prepared for Test cricket in his remote, intemperate, South Island hometown. He had replied that net pitches in Motueka prepared one for anything.

Opener John Wright was soon out though without adding to his overnight score of 55. He attempted to drive Ian Botham on to the on side, a full yard out of his crease, but was rapped on the pads. The appeal was upheld, and Wright's debut innings had come to an end. Botham bowled well throughout the innings, but the whole of the day's operation hinged on Chris Old. When Willis had John Parker caught at backward short leg by Brian Rose, 191 for 4 soon became 196 for 8. Old had taken four wickets for one run in 20 balls in which three of those were caught behind by wicket-keeper Bob Taylor, the first from a nick from Lees, resulting in a superb right-hand catch far to his right. Taylor's second catch was taken when Bev Congdon, on 44, drove firm-footed at a ball which left him off the pitch. Shortly after, Taylor dived low to his right to dismiss Dayle Hadlee.

Richard Hadlee, meanwhile, who had inherited much more of the batting talent from the Hadlees' illustrious father, Walter Hadlee, played some stirring strokes off Willis after lunch. Richard Collinge, however, soon fell after playing over a ball from Old and then Stephen Boock was bowled to give Botham another deserved wicket. The New Zealanders were all out for 228, with Old taking 6 for 54, with two wickets apiece for Willis and Botham. England seamer Chris Old had delivered some of the best bowling of his career. He had bowled a short expensive spell before lunch, downwind, and had struggled. So, after much deliberation with Boycott, he decided to switch ends. A howling gale blew straight down the ground, Old was superb and bowling into the wind took those six wickets!

England had to dig in and they had the best person placed to undertake the task in Geoff Boycott. The New Zealand bowling was never quite approaching the tightness of England's, but it was enough to keep Boycott to just 20 runs in his first two and a half hours. The pitch began showing signs of uneven bounce and as it dried, lost its pace. It was becoming more straightforward. Boycott survived an early appeal for a catch at the wicket and an even louder one for lbw. Eventually he hooked and cut successive balls from Richard Hadlee for four; the first dropped just short of long leg and the second just cleared the leaping slips. He luckily remained at the crease. Meanwhile, Brian Rose glanced a ball from Collinge off his pads to be beautifully caught by wicket-keeper Lees, and Geoff Miller, having batted well on his elevation in the order, fell in the last over playing across a slow full toss, without violent intent, and missed. Rose had presented Collinge with his 100th Test wicket, Miller giving left-arm spinner Boock his first. England finished on 89 for 2, still trailing by 139.

England's progress on the third day was slow. In fact, very slow and this was down to one batsman in particular, Geoffrey Boycott. Many who witnessed his ultra-cautious 77 thought it was counterproductive. England's batting as a whole approached catastrophic standards and after the first innings was in danger of getting the order of the Wellington boot at the Basin Reserve. It was only Boycott who held the batting together in his singular, depressing way. He batted 442 minutes and faced 302 balls on a typically English pitch which offered little movement. His nearest contributor was Graham Roope with 37 and when Boycott was sixth out with the score on 188, the innings collapsed. With 38 runs overnight to his credit, Boycott's hourly progress on the third day was 10, 12, 6 (including a savage square cut for four) and 12. In that time night watchman Bob Taylor, Derek Randall and Roope were dismissed. How much pressure was Boycott arguably placing on the other batsmen by his dismal scoring rate? Also, how much encouragement did the bowlers have at the sight of more crease occupation by the opposition's number one batsman?

England's first fifty took 185 minutes and the first hour after lunch yielded just 23 runs. Meanwhile, Derek Randall's lack of success since his 174 in the Centenary Test in Melbourne was becoming distinctly discouraging to both himself and his team. Randall fell for 4, caught by Mark Burgess off Richard Hadlee. Graham Roope's six boundaries included a classic off-drive and his 110-minute innings was all too briefly promising. The last five wickets disappeared in a gloomy epilogue for 32. England had been dismissed for 215 handing New Zealand a first innings-lead of 13.

Dick Brittenden described the day as, 'England advanced with the unexciting inevitability of a Caterpillar tractor, driven by a Boycott who treated the task with the gravest suspicion.'

The New Zealand openers, John Wright and Robert Anderson, survived five overs from Bob Willis and Mike Hendrick before the close, New Zealand finishing day three on 12 for 0. The New Zealanders were well placed to attempt to push on and try and win their first ever Test against England.

Much depended on how the pitch would last out in the remaining two days of the Test with England captain Geoff Boycott calling it 'an interesting stage'. There was some encouragement for the spinners and England, now having put the New Zealanders in to bat, were beginning to get concerned about batting last. The wicket had seen encroachment by both sets of bowlers on both sides.

Richard Collinge, bowling left-arm over the wicket, had trouble with his follow-through and had already bowled at both ends in the match. He had created a patch seven feet in front of the popping crease, which was roughly on a good length for a fast bowler. Collinge had already been warned by the umpires in the game. England now feared that, although most of the pitch would not deteriorate, albeit remaining of uneven bounce and pace, the patches might become increasingly awkward by the final day. However, New Zealand's Mark Burgess knew that 'Their bowlers will be at us very hard'.

The rest day saw a few of the New Zealand batsmen deciding to undertake some practice. Soon it developed into a turnout of ten of the squad, the only absentees being Richard Collinge, who had to go to Masterton for the day, and Dayle Hadlee who was receiving physiotherapy treatment. Hadlee had suffered severely-pulled muscles in his left side during Saturday's play.

The weather forecast for the last two days of the Test seemed fairly positive, but there were pitch problems caused by the bowlers of both sides. In delivering the ball, the footmarks left by the bowlers had created extensive wear to the pitch. Some of the bowlers had left marks just about in line with the stumps.

Who would have thought that only two wickets would fall before lunch on the fourth day for 63 runs, and no fewer than 17 wickets would fall for 101 runs in the next sensational four hours! Bob Willis was the main destroyer, and was making a case to becoming a potential match-winner. From his seventh ball after lunch to his fifth ball in the sixth over, he was to dismiss five batsmen; Geoff Howarth, Bev Congdon, John Parker, Mark Burgess and Richard Hadlee. It was a depressing scenario for New Zealand with Willis ably supported by some great catching from the English fielders. Willis ended with 5 for 32 as Mike Hendrick and Ian Botham took two wickets apiece. Opener Anderson top scored for the hosts, with just 26.

The home side had been dismissed for 123 and it left England to score just 137 to win the Test. One nameless player stated, 'If we can't get 137 to win, we ought to be shipped back home.'

With many in the media being very critical of Geoff Boycott after the third day's play for being ultra-cautious and counter-productive, they were now beginning to regret their words. In the second over, Boycott, attempting a drive, was bowled off his pads by Richard Collinge, giving the bowler his 500th first-class wicket. It had taken New Zealand eight minutes to get that first wicket. A mighty roar went up around the ground 'stifling the vigorous traffic noises which always enliven cricket at the Basin Reserve', wrote reporter Brittenden.

Brittenden was to pass away in June 2002 aged 82 and was to recall about his reporting life that, 'If I single out one moment it is (Richard) Collinge bowling (Geoff) Boycott off stick for one to start England's collapse in Wellington in 1978.'

Boycott then sat back and watched as Collinge and Richard Hadlee wreaked havoc amongst the English batsmen, in what was surely the most emotional 19 overs delivered in New Zealand's cricketing history. Boycott's dismissal was celebrated by a streaker and soon after Geoff Miller was out trying to avoid a rearing a ball from Collinge, caught by Anderson. Two batsmen back in the hutch for eight. Ten runs later Derek Randall, stretching forward, was given out leg before also to Collinge and, with no score added, Graham Roope snicked a catch behind off Hadlee. Ian Botham then decided to go on the attack with some excellent drives and square cuts bringing an element of hope to the proceedings. But after he hooked a four, Hadlee reinforced his leg-side field, bowled the inevitable short pitcher and Botham was caught in the trap. He had made 19 and England were now 38 for 5. Boock ran out a surprised Bob Taylor to make it 38 for 6 and with the score on 53 both Chris Old and Mike Hendrick became victims of Hadlee.

In fact, when Hendrick was out at 5.52pm with the total on 53, he became only the second man to make a Test pair against New Zealand.

Bob Willis, meanwhile, went back to the hotel to have a bath 'as I was so stiff after bowling in a typical Wellington wind' but was hastily summoned back with the score on 38 for 6.

The close of play had arrived and England, on 53 for 8, were still 84 runs short of victory. At this point Boycott stated, 'Now will people understand why I bat slowly!'

It had been a woeful batting display with England looking like a depressed county outfit. New Zealand were simply inspired, team and crowd alike. The scene had been set for an historic final day at the Basin Reserve; it had taken 48 Tests and 48 years for New Zealand to beat England, and now they were on the threshold.

It did not take long for New Zealand to wrap up their historic victory with England only adding 11 to their overnight score. They had been dismissed for 64, giving the New Zealanders victory by 72 runs. Richard Hadlee finished with 6 for 26, Richard Collinge 3 for 35.

It had been an amazing turnaround. When the players came off the pitch the previous day at tea the New Zealand players and supporters felt they had lost the match. It was a great feeling for Richard Hadlee, the bowler of the match, achieving what his father, Walter Hadlee, former captain and now chairman of the Cricket Council, had tried to do since 1937. At the end of the game the crowd cheered Mark Burgess and his team and sang 'For they are jolly good fellows'.

Bert Sutcliffe presented the individual $150 awards to New Zealand players John Wright (for batting), Richard Hadlee (bowling) and Warren Lees (fielding). An emotional Sutcliffe recalled that it had been his greatest ambition to play in a winning Test team, but it had not been realised. Moments later several New Zealand players relished the occasion with glasses of sparkling wine.

Sutcliffe, writing in the official programmes for the Tests whilst secretary of the Rothman Foundation, sponsors of the Test Series, had written, 'Thirty-one years ago, almost to the day, I was launched into the Test arena at Lancaster Park, against England, led by the late Walter Hammond, one of England's greatest players. I am happy to recall an opening partnership of 116 with my New Zealand captain Walter Hadlee, but later, sad to say, I blotted my copybook by dropping my first catch, offered by none other than Walter Hammond. That baptism was a wonderful experience thanks to the England players of 1947. Today, some enthusiasts are saying that this could be New Zealand's greatest chance to win her first ever Test against England – when they do I will help them celebrate. But England bring much professional experience which is hard to match when the chips are down.'

For the third Test, Sutcliffe wrote in the programme that New Zealand's victory in Wellington had been 'their finest hour'.

Bob Taylor, later, would recall that there were no excuses and that the wicket was sporting, but nothing more than that. It had been a mad afternoon in which Richard Hadlee had bowled superbly.

Afterwards, Geoff Boycott faced a barrage of questions. Did his responsibilities inhibit his own batting? 'To some degree,' he replied. 'It is similar to batting for Yorkshire for some years. One is conscious of the situation.' Could England save the series by winning one of the two remaining Tests? 'I am a rational and sensible guy. I say there is little between the teams since England lost players to the World Series in Australia. Our strength is in bowling and fielding. That was borne out in the context of the Test. New Zealand players and supporters felt at tea on the fourth day that they had lost the match. There was a resigned silence when we came off the field. Yet at the end of the next two hours, everyone was experiencing the thrill and the excitement of the New Zealand win. That was how completely the game changed. There were opportunities for either side to win.'

New Zealand photographer John Selkirk, on looking back on that eventful fifth day, recalls, 'As to my memories of the fifth day of the first Test. It's a bit hazy, but I do remember being a bit worried about the weather. It wasn't a great forecast and it dawned overcast threatening to rain, but it held off luckily. I think New Zealand only needed a couple of wickets and it was all over quite quickly. I set up my 800mm lens on its tripod high up on the stand at the Basin. I wanted to be in a position to see the whole wicket and knew the players would be coming my way. I was 26-years-old at the time and had been covering cricket since 1971. It was fascinating to see the reaction from the smallish crowd there and the adulation piled on our greatest ever cricketer Richard Hadlee. In those days there was no problem mingling with the players and moving through their dressing rooms, etc. Geoff Boycott held an impromptu press conference with Ken Barrington in the England dressing room and I caught a nice picture of Ian Botham and Stephen Boock having a chat. Champagne was flowing with the New Zealand team during the celebrations.'

Ken Barrington, the England tour manager, offered no comforts for the quick recovery of England's lost standards. 'I think we have to face the fact we are going to have a hard time for the next two to three years. I went on an MCC "A" Tour and it was an immense benefit to me. It served as a training ground for Test level for several of the side. Another Under-25 party went to Pakistan in 1967 which also produced England players of good quality.' Barrington was speaking with the intention of recommending overseas tours for selected young players as the first practical step towards finding batsmen of genuine class. Barrington had seen England fail against the spin in Pakistan and now the pace of Richard Hadlee and Richard Collinge in Wellington. The previous lowest total of 181, at Christchurch in 1929/30, would have brought a comfortable victory in Wellington.

After a day of travelling and rest, England headed down to the south-east of the South Island for their next tour match at Carisbrook, in Dunedin, against Otago. The ground, more famous as a venue for New Zealand rugby games, had hosted just six Test matches up to the tourists' visit and two of those, in 1955 and 1966, had been against England. The ground was the main home for Otago and one of the earliest recorded first-class matches held there had been in February 1884 against the touring Tasmanians.

Otago captain and wicket-keeper Warren Lees won the toss and decided to bat. The Carisbrook pitch was green enough at the start, however, to whet the appetite of England's fast bowlers, Mike Hendrick, John Lever and Ian Botham. They ended up having a field day and between them bowled out batsmen who were not equal to the movement off the seam and through the air.

In fact, if half of the passes outside the off stump had made contact, Otago would have been routed. As it was, it needed the last four to double the total to a modest 130.

England's left-arm pace man John Lever, who took 5 for 59, and wicket-keeper Paul Downton had both made major contributions. Downton was making a rare tour appearance and performed immaculately in taking six catches. Lever, who had been left out of the Wellington Test partly due to a fitness doubt, proved there should be no qualms for the second Test starting in eight day's time. With his awkward line of left-arm over the wicket he proved he was more likely to be a wicket-taker than Mike Hendrick. Lever provided a good variety of line and length and had a good record since winning his position on merit, in India, the winter before. Three of Lever's wickets were caught at the wicket, Paul Facoory and Lance Cairns beautifully held by 20-year-old Paul Downton. He went a long way to vindicating his surprise selection. Carisbrook provided the evidence of Downton's outstanding natural ability which had immeasurably benefitted from being around a fine mentor in Bob Taylor. Along with Lever's 5 for 59, which was spoilt in one over by Lance Cairns who hit a swept six, Botham took 3 for 33 and Hendrick 2 for 25.

In reply to Otago's 130, England closed on 58 for 0, Geoff Boycott and Derek Randall cruising along without being in any difficulty.

However, in stark contrast, day two saw England dithering and bumbling along and the fall of Boycott's wicket in the morning session foreshadowed the difficulties to come. Boycott was out for 37 caught behind by Lees, prodding at a ball from

Brian McKechnie, who was moving the ball around, especially away from the bat. With figures of 3 for 46, McKechnie, also a New Zealand rugby international, did himself proud.

Lance Cairns proved a most able partner to McKechnie and more frequently moved the ball into the batsmen. His medium pace resulted in tremendous bowling, taking 4 for 73 off 42 overs. Clive Radley's dreadful lack of form saw him fall lbw to Cairns for 44, with more elegance shown by Graham Roope for his 28. At no stage in the innings did the expected authority of the England batsmen materialise. England were finally all out for 195, a paltry lead of 65. Botham claimed two Otago wickets before the end of the day, Wayne Blair and Paul Facoory, with all of the batsmen playing and missing a lot. With Otago 41 for 2 and on a pitch of variable bounce, it was hard to imagine Otago scoring enough for England to lose the game. Unless the last day came alight, it was shaping up to be a match that would easily be forgotten.

Ian Botham continued where he left off on day three and at one stage had figures of 4 for 9 in 9.3 overs. He finished with 7 for 58 with Otago bowled out for 146. This meant England required 82 in fifty minutes and the arbitrary 15 eight-ball overs.

As usual, Geoff Boycott was over-cautious in his determination to get England off to a good start and in fifty minutes and ten overs only seventeen runs were scored, which left 65 to get in 15 overs. Derek Randall and Graham Roope immediately upped the pace until Roope lunged at Graeme Thomson and was leg before with the score on 53, in the 11th over. An over later Randall, on 28, drove Lance Cairns to Stu McCullum (father of Brendon, the future New Zealand Test captain) fielding at long off. Clive Radley then smacked one four before driving back to the persevering Thomson and England were left requiring 12 off 18 balls. It was proving to be an undignified scramble to win, but one that favoured the grafting batsmen.

Thomson then bowled two bouncers at Botham, the second of which was brilliantly hooked to the square leg boundary, however, it was left to Mike Gatting to win the game in the penultimate over with two boundaries, a lofted drive and a controlled cut off Cairns. England had won by six wickets with ten balls remaining.

The victory was a rarity on the tour. Otago were condemned to share the fate of the North West Governor's XI near the Khyber Pass, who also lost a first-class game to England earlier in the tour. Another was tied in New Plymouth and England had lost the first Test in Wellington.

The rest were draws on the bad surfaces of Pakistan and New Zealand, though at Carisbrook, in Dunedin, the ball seamed at an uneven height, which was exactly what England did not want in the short space between the humiliation of Wellington and the forthcoming second Test in Christchurch.

The day after the victory at Carisbrook, England began their three-day tour match against Young New Zealand, in the small town of Temuka in the Canterbury plains. The town is located 200 kilometres north of Dunedin and is situated on the south-east coast of the South Island. The match between the sides at the Temuka Oval would be the first ever first-class game played on the ground. The first match at the Oval had been back in 1884, when the Temuka Cricket Club, who played in the South Canterbury league, had played its first match.

England won the toss and elected to bat on another doubtful pitch, which had been prepared by a local policeman, and bore the common fault of New Zealand surfaces, by being two-paced and of variable bounce. In the sixth over, Geoff Boycott had a delivery from Martin Snedden which 'stopped' and he was out, caught at short leg by Doug Bracewell for 5.

After his low score, Boycott, grim faced, got Mike Gatting and Paul Downton, instead of playing a scheduled game of golf, to bowl to him in the nets that afternoon, running them about, tiring them out for nearly two hours.

The session ended with an assortment of local schoolchildren also joining in! Once again Boycott was showing his dedicated side.

Brian Rose's hope for a long innings didn't materialise when the ball hurried through and he fell leg before to Doug Bracewell for 17. Bracewell then had Clive Radley caught off his glove by Evan Gray at slip and England found themselves 78 for 3.

In these difficult conditions Derek Randall, desperate for a personal boost of confidence before the last two Tests, struggled to find his touch. Often his sweep didn't work and he got himself into a tangle of wrong positions. Gradually, with the help of Graham Roope – often at his best against spin – Randall's timing improved and he was able to cut convincingly, hitting firmly to leg and drive when the few opportunities came for shots in front of the wicket on a slow turner. After three hours of toil and hard work he reached his 50 and his stand with Roope, caught at short leg off bat and pad again by Doug Bracewell off his brother Brendon, was worth 104 in 131 minutes.

Roope had produced some dazzling shots, a straight drive for six against the slow left arm of Evan Gray, and a back-foot drive off the All Blacks rugby footballer Brian McKechnie which any batsman would have been proud to have played anywhere at any time. Randall also slogged a six, which took him to 94, off an outrageous long hop bowled by the Test all-rounder Jeremy Coney. The previous ball bowled by Coney had gone through so slowly that Randall had almost completed his shot by the time it had arrived, and he was lucky not to have been caught at square leg. The nineties, however, became torturous for Randall and when on 99 he was given out to an appeal for a catch at the wicket off the promising 18-year-old fast bowler Brendon Bracewell; however, wicket-keeper 'Jock' Edwards, another Test player, at once pointed out that the ball had not carried. The umpire, after conferring with his colleague, rescinded the decision and justice was done. At last, Randall's luck had changed and his century had come in 340 minutes and included ten boundaries.

The century which had eluded Randall since the 174 he scored in the Melbourne Centenary Test the previous March finally arrived in the idyllic settings the game was being played in. His general form had been so erratic, his anxieties so pronounced, that until this revival of his fortunes it seemed a sympathetic act to omit him for the forthcoming second Test. Not now. He ended the day 103 not out with Geoff Miller on 13 and England closing on 229 for 4.

England batted on to reach 310 on day two, scoring in an undistinguished manner, adding a further 81 runs to their overnight score. Spinner Evan Gray ended with 4 for 58 whilst Doug Bracewell finished with 4 for 87.

The rest of the day was then dominated by the spin of Geoff Miller and Phil Edmonds, who were able to have a long and successful bowl. Miller was productive with his off-breaks and it was only Brian McKechnie who momentarily mastered him. He hit Miller for four sixes, but after the fourth Miller got his revenge and McKechnie, on 33, was caught in the crowded short leg position by Graham Roope. Once Edmonds found a more accurate line, both he and Miller constantly rapped the pads used as a second line of defence and with a modicum of luck would have improved on their records. Miller finished with 5 for 63 and Edmonds two for 24 off 18 overs, but they were not likely to figure as central bowlers in the remaining two Tests. New Zealand Test pitches seemed to be more suited to an endless belt of fast and seam bowling.

The consistent batting of left-hander Bruce Edgar, from Wellington, held the innings together. Edgar was eventually dismissed by a shrewd piece of anticipation by Edmonds at short leg. Almost as soon as the stroke was being made, Edmonds moved into the position and made a difficult catch look absurdly easy. The next two runs saw the disappearance of John Reid and Auckland wicket-keeper 'Jock' Edwards. This knocked the stuffing out of the resistance of the youngsters and with Martin Snedden falling to the penultimate ball of the day, caught Roope bowled Miller, Young New Zealand finished 189 behind with one wicket remaining on 129 for 9.

Ten runs were added on day three before Geoff Miller had Brendon Bracewell caught and bowled, ending with excellent figures of 6 for 71. Young New Zealand had been asked to follow on, 171 runs behind. It was Miller's best bowling figures on the tour since his 6 for 62 on the rain-affected pitch at Rawalpindi in the first game of the tour.

In the second innings he was no less destructive with his off-breaks, collecting four of the first seven wickets to go, for only 42. Miller turned the ball appreciably and his natural flight and consistency had the batsmen searching for the precise length. His match figures of 10 for 124 did not flatter him.

When the last 15 eight-ball overs began, Young New Zealand were 136 for 7 and with Doug Bracewell and Evan Gray defending so stubbornly that captain Boycott had to turn to Lever. In no time the game had been won, with Lever taking the remaining three wickets in seven deliveries in the third and fifth overs at a personal cost of two runs. Lever's final figures were 4 for 44 whilst Miller's were 4 for 53. Young New Zealand had been dismissed for 148 and England had won by an innings and 23 runs, their most emphatic win of the whole tour to date.

The hospitality and friendliness of the locals in Temuka left a big impression on the tourists. During their stay they were treated like lords. The ladies who provided the lunches for the three-day game produced a table that would have compared with any leading hotel in the world. Fresh salmon, turkeys, hams and a roast suckling pig virtually outshone the cricket, such was the excellence of the food.

Despite the two victories since the Wellington debacle England still went into the second Test as underdogs. However, the New Zealand captain Mark Burgess was unlikely to play; a broken finger on his right hand meant that he could not hold a bat. Another blow for the hosts was the news that Dayle Hadlee, their seamer, had a strained back and was also very doubtful.

Australian Ian Chappell was in the country and stated that if New Zealand could dismiss Geoff Boycott cheaply, England would also lose the next two Tests!

The England selectors on tour, Boycott, tour manager Ken Barrington and vice captain Bob Willis, now had a selection headache, attempting to balance the side between the bowling and trying to squeeze as many runs as possible from the Christchurch pitch that was expected to be green and receptive to pace and seam.

Boycott and company, though, were probably sure that three of the 17-man squad would not take part, spinner Geoff Cope, batsman Mike Gatting and reserve wicket-keeper Paul Downton.

7

The tour concludes in Auckland

Ian Botham had come in and thrown the bat and then called his captain for a quick single. Boycott, having advanced a few yards, then sent him back, but Botham in full cry was not to be halted and charged past his captain before the wicket had been broken.

THE following day, after the victory over Young New Zealand, England returned to nearby Christchurch for the second Test, which was being played at the same ground where they had drawn their three-day tour match against Canterbury.

It was a quiet eve of the Test for England who named a squad of 13, but the build-up to the Test had proved more of an anxious time for the hosts. Mark Burgess, the New Zealand captain, who had broken his right forefinger, had come through a batting trial and his chances of playing in the game were looking good. With reports that Burgess did not quite have

117

full batting power in his hand, questions were being asked as to whether he would field at second slip, where he had already taken a number of good catches. Bruce Edgar, who played for Young New Zealand in Temuka, was on standby in case Burgess had to withdraw. Dayle Hadlee, however, had not recovered from his back injury and Ewen Chatfield, who was already in the 12, would take his place.

England decided on leaving out birthday boys John Lever and Geoff Cope from their side. Geoffrey Boycott won the toss and decided to bat and with England soon crumbling to 26 for 3, probably wished he hadn't. Boycott was first man out when a fast break back delivery from Richard Collinge kept low and rapped him on the pads. Derek Randall lasted seven balls and fell for a duck, snicking a delivery from Richard Hadlee low to Mark Burgess at second slip. Then first change bowler Ewen Chatfield had Brian Rose caught brilliantly by Geoff Howarth diving at leg slip, but the batting collapse was soon thwarted by Graham Roope and Geoff Miller. The New Zealand team were buoyant after Wellington and had now relieved themselves of the psychological handicap of never having beaten England in a Test. By the time Roope and Miller had started on their 77-run stand, some of the cutting edge had been blunted. Twice Roope escaped. The first was a hard fourth slip catch to Bob Anderson off Collinge when only on 4, and the second was even harder, to Hadlee at gully from Chatfield when on 27. Roope and Miller did their country proud in stopping the rot.

When Miller was on 31 he played an early hook shot off Collinge and as he finished the stroke he felt the ball crack into his cheek below his right ear. Miller soon found himself falling to the ground in agony. He was taken to hospital where, luckily, an X-ray showed no break, and he was later able to join in the birthday party held for Lever and Cope.

The short-pitched deliveries and bouncers that the bowlers were able to get away with were questionable, especially those bowled by Richard Hadlee and ignored by umpire Bob Monteith. There were four bowled in one over, three in the next and then Roope was caught off another short-pitched delivery with the first ball of the following over.

Roope had gone for 50 and the recipient of the catch was once again Mark Burgess at second slip, showing no signs of discomfort despite his injured finger. Eight balls previously debutant Clive Radley had been on 15 when he gloved a short-pitched delivery from Hadlee to wicket-keeper Warren Lees. With Roope and Radley now back in the pavilion England were 128 for 5. The entire day had seen the ball banged in short of a length and eventually, when the first attack was spent, Bev Congdon contributed 18 defensive overs in succession for a mere 14 runs.

Ian Botham and Bob Taylor comfortably held out against the second new ball when, significantly, Richard Hadlee had run out of steam. England closed on 172 for 5.

As Botham strode to the crease, windmilling his bat, Richard Hadlee smirked. Dick Collinge apparently stated to the young all-rounder, 'Oh yeah, son, you and whose army?'

Earlier in the month Ian Botham had made 126 on the same ground against Canterbury. This time, however, Botham and Bob Taylor began day two by having to restrain themselves against some eccentric bounce. After lunch Botham set about left-arm spinner Stephen Boock, driving him over mid-off for six.

The going was never easy for Botham and Taylor, a partnership which had begun on 128 for 5 when Geoff Miller departed for hospital. It increased steadily until 160 had been added in six hours and forty minutes with Botham moving on to 99. Ewen Chatfield then pinned the Somerset all-rounder down with a very tidy over and, as it neared completion, provoked Botham into trying for a quick single to Collinge, who was not noted for his athletic prowess in the field, at wide mid-on. Collinge, however, successfully threw down the stumps and Taylor, who had not made his ground, was run out for 45. On departing he went out of his way to reassure his young batting partner. England were 288 for 6.

Botham's historic maiden Test century soon followed, of which many more were to come. He had already shown, in his short career to date, that he was well on the way to becoming the best all-rounder England had seen for many a year.

Botham was now ready to attack in earnest, but on 103 was caught at the wicket, projecting a huge blow off the back foot at a ball from Boock, which lifted.

Mike Brearley had arrived in New Zealand from England to rejoin the tour, not as a squad member, but reporting for a Sunday newspaper. After his worries about Botham many months earlier at the first net session in Rawalpindi, he now witnessed the Somerset youngster's maiden Test century. Brearley was not only astonished, but delighted by what he had seen. Reporting on Botham's innings he stated, 'an extraordinary ability, staggering . . . he isn't afraid, he explores his own limits; he might play Test matches as if he were in a club game, but he is patently not just an ordinary boy from Yeovil.'

Botham's dismissal brought Chris Old to the crease. Old played two on-drives for four before playing across a delivery from Hadlee and was bowled for 8. Phil Edmonds was next in. At Wellington in the first Test he had been ranked by the umpires as an 'unrecognised' batsman and must not have bouncers bowled at him. Edmonds soon effortlessly drove Hadlee over mid-off for four. This was enough for Hadlee to disregard previous rulings and bowl at him short and fast which resulted in Edmonds hooking him for six. Hadlee was now fuming, bowling another bouncer which Edmonds hooked for four, and ended by taking 18 off Hadlee's over and ten off his next, which included a classic drive through the covers. For a highly competent batsman, Edmonds had been grossly unlucky on the tour. He had got out to brilliant catches, unplayable balls and questionable decisions and had made only 45 runs in nine innings. Now he had made 50 out of 70 runs in seventy minutes, which included eight fours and a six. With exactly an hour to go to the close, Edmonds lost his wicket and there was then widespread apprehension amongst the locals at what the last fifty minutes might bring to the New Zealand batsmen after a weary eleven hours in the field. However, there was no declaration, with Geoff Miller and Bob Willis batting through the last hour scoring just 19 runs with England closing on the highly commendable score of 394 for 9. Miller, having resumed his innings after retiring hurt, ended the day on 66 not out.

Geoff Miller and Bob Willis added a further 24 runs on the morning of the third day before Miller was caught by Bev Congdon off Richard Collinge for 89 to leave England 418 all out.

Phil Edmonds then found himself thrown into the bowling attack quite early on to partner Ian Botham, after the opening spell from Bob Willis and Chris Old had found no success. Edmonds soon had John Wright caught and bowled off a full toss for 4 and when Bob Willis returned to have Geoff Howarth caught off his glove, a dolly to Edmonds at short square leg, New Zealand were 52 for 2. Opener Bob Anderson was going along nicely having played an exciting innings, but when he had reached 62 he was involved in an incident which was to overshadow the day's other proceedings. With the score on 82 for 2, Anderson had his leg bail clipped off the bowling of Edmonds. Wicket-keeper Bob Taylor, standing up, had his appeal immediately endorsed by umpire Fred Goodall, a decision proved correct by television playbacks. But home captain and non-striker Mark Burgess did not appear convinced and swished his hat in apparent anger. Anderson was equally confused, and as he departed, Burgess went over to England skipper Geoffrey Boycott at mid-wicket. Boycott then spoke to Taylor and the fielders close to the bat and told Burgess, 'If Bob Taylor says he was out, he was out.' Barrackers in the crowd began their chants of 'Cheats, Cheats, Cheats' with the Poms' parental legitimacy also being questioned. Later, a shirtless spectator accosted square leg umpire Bob Monteith and gestured to Taylor that he had knocked the bail off with his pads. Anybody who knew Taylor would dismiss such a charge as absurd.

Burgess, however, was not satisfied and complained that Ian Botham was creating a patch on the leg stump with his follow-through. He also told the umpire that Phil Edmonds was fielding too close at forward short leg for the fast bowling of Bob Willis. Before play was resumed, Botham was warned not to encroach on the forbidden area. And then, off the first ball from Willis, a 'no ball' was called because Edmonds was, according to the law, too close to the batsman and had moved during the run-up. Boycott asked Edmonds to keep perfectly still, which he did, and there were no further complaints. Bev Congdon's reaction was amusingly candid. 'It takes me all my time to watch the ball without bothering about anything else,' he said.

Congdon's seventy-minute effort, which ended the suspicion that he might have nicked the ball on to his pads, soon came to an end when on 20. He was given out, leg before, to a delivery from Botham that kept low and broke back. It epitomised New Zealand's struggle to deny England the match and retain the 1-0 lead in the three-match series. Bad light rescued New Zealand with the hosts ending the day on 122 for 4.

The rest day of the Test saw the tourists spending a day power-boating up a river in Canterbury where local farmers took out members of both teams. A memorable day was finished off in style with a barbecue and a 'swimming party'. It had been a day to savour and remember for the squad with the arid landscape of Pakistan, earlier in the tour, becoming a distant memory.

The first seventy minutes on day four saw New Zealand struggle to muster the 97 runs still needed to avoid the follow-on and it went generally as predicted. Burgess and Parker survived for half an hour, with difficulty, then three wickets quickly fell. Burgess, driving firm-footed at Botham, was caught at second slip by Graham Roope and Warren Lees, in Botham's next over, was beautifully caught at silly point by Geoff Miller at full stretch, apparently off bat and arm. Hadlee played back and missed a good-length ball from Edmonds, which bowled him. It looked like New Zealand, now at 153 for 7, might be batting again before lunch, but with the arrival of Richard Collinge at number nine, things began to look different. Freed of the concern that anyone might bowl short at him, he took a step back towards leg slip as the ball was bowled and surged into action off both the back and front foot.

John Parker eventually began to play well after surviving two chances off Botham when on 10 and 19. Collinge and Parker put on 58 runs with a flourish, but with eight needed to avoid the follow-on, Collinge then lost his wicket when he turned Botham to Edmonds at backward short leg. Stephen Boock held out for twenty-seven minutes in which just five runs were scored, but then fell, caught at the wicket off Edmonds. Parker now had to take control and soon he scored the three runs needed to make England bat again. He finally ended on 53 not out when Ewen Chatfield was caught by Edmonds off Botham. Edmonds in taking the catch had claimed his fourth of the innings! New Zealand had been dismissed for 235, and trailed England by 183.

England's second innings began with Geoff Boycott and out-of-form Brian Rose scoring only 25 in eighty minutes before Rose was caught behind by Lees off Collinge for 7. After the turgid start to the innings it seemed as though a plan was in place for Boycott to hold one end, while his partners attacked vigorously at the other. After a good start and looking like the Derek Randall of old, Ewen Chatfield ended a long run-up by breaking Randall's wicket without warning. Randall was far out of his ground, but the absence of the previous warning, which was considered ethical if the breaking of the wicket be done at all, left a sour taste, by no means only on the England side. Just before Randall's misfortune, Richard Hadlee had pointed out from mid-off, though not to the victim himself, that Randall was backing up over-eagerly. After the controversial decision, with Randall having been run out for 13, Boycott was soon to follow, also run out, having scored 26. Ian Botham had come in and had begun to attack the bowling in his swashbuckling style. Looking to push the score on, he then called his captain for a quick single. Boycott, having advanced a few yards, sent him back, but Botham, in full cry, was not to be halted and charged past his captain before the wicket had been broken. Botham did not let the run-out affect him and hit 30 off 31 balls by the close. England finished the day on 96 for 4, a lead of 279 with one day remaining.

England began day five by declaring on their overnight score, so leaving them a full day to bowl New Zealand out and draw level in the series. Six balls into the innings, Bob Willis struck, having John Wright caught at second slip by Graham Roope, for a duck, which was soon followed by Geoff Howarth caught at short square leg by Phil Edmonds off Chris Old. The match was once again creating controversy as umpire Fred Goodall warned both Bob Willis and Ian Botham over their follow-throughs, which led to a dispute with skipper Geoffrey Boycott. Both were warned for running down the pitch in the forbidden area and with the danger of losing his key quickies for the match, Boycott argued that the patches were as a result of four days of 'wear by all of the right-arm over the wicket bowlers'. After Willis had his final warning he turned to Boycott and said despairingly, 'You might as well take me off.' Boycott told him to go round the wicket.

Skipper Mark Burgess then allowed a short-pitched delivery from Willis to strike him on his left elbow, standing upright and taking the ball like a stoic. Bev Congdon was miraculously picked up left-handed at third slip by Botham, out for a duck, off Willis and New Zealand were now 19 for 3. Next over, Willis had both Robert Anderson and Warren Lees bowled off stump with successive deliveries. Ten balls had seen three wickets fall and an unfortunate accident, which was as good as a wicket. The rest was academic with Richard Hadlee bravely hitting eight boundaries. When he fell ninth down having scored 39, New Zealand had collapsed to 95 for 9. Ewen Chatfield, booed by some, applauded by others, for running out Derek Randall without warning when backing up, was last out to Botham, who had completed a wonderful display.

It had been a swift and sweeping victory that day at Lancaster Park, with the New Zealand innings having lasted only 172 minutes and 27 overs! It was a supreme triumph for Geoff Boycott, totally vindicated in all his tactical decisions, and it had been a stunning success for Ian Botham.

He had made 103, then 30 in 36 balls after being given licence to thrill, took 5 for 73 and 3 for 38, plus three outstanding second-innings catches. A dazzling career lay ahead for the Somerset all-rounder.

Boycott celebrated his first victory as England captain and said, 'I was surprised New Zealand were bowled out in under three hours. To do so was magnificent. It took New Zealand about the same time to bowl us out at Wellington, but as Christchurch was a far better pitch, it was a far greater achievement.'

Mike Brearley was not impressed by Geoffrey Boycott's captaincy in Christchurch, which was going to go a long way to him never captaining his country again. Bob Willis, who was now vice captain, described how Boycott was unable to force the pace when England needed quick runs for a declaration in their second innings.

Willis sensibly sent Ian Botham in at number four. But when Boycott was run out 'by about 16 yards' he came back to the dressing room where he 'sat in a corner' with a towel over his head. Phil Edmonds asked Boycott about the rest of the batting order and he said that it now appeared to be the responsibility of the vice captain. Next day he was still sulking. Willis later stated he presumed that Boycott would be declaring at the overnight score to give England a complete day to bowl New Zealand out and square the series. At the time Boycott had no intention of declaring as having seen England already losing one Test, did not want to see them lose another. He did declare, though, and Willis and Botham did most of the damage as the New Zealanders were dismissed for 105. Some say the tour went a long way in ending Boycott's chances of ever captaining his country again.

Wicket-keeper Bob Taylor had enjoyed working with his understudy Paul Downton on the winter tour. Taylor took Downton under his wing and they had, during the course of the tour, lengthy chats about technique and the atmosphere of playing for England abroad. Taylor was impressed by Downton's hunger to learn. When Downton took over from Taylor against the West Indians in 1984, Taylor knew that Downton had deserved his place. The teams would now head to Eden Park, Auckland on the North Island for the third Test, a six-day decider.

England would finish their tour of New Zealand as they had started it, by playing at Eden Park. The whole winter tour had been a mammoth undertaking, and that first tour match in Rawalpindi on 30 November must have seemed like a lifetime ago, not only to the players and management, but even the media that had followed them. The tourists went into the final tour match of the series with the Kiwis all square. What could they conjure up in the third Test, which was to be played over six days?

Mark Burgess won the toss and decided to bat on a pitch far milder than the other two Test pitches in Wellington and Christchurch. England had implied that there would be changes by naming a squad of 13 for the Test. Mike Gatting came in for Brian Rose, but the selectors decided that Derek Randall, and not Geoff Miller, would open with Geoff Boycott. John Lever came in, replacing Chris Old. Some would have liked to have seen both Lever and Old included and a batsman left out, especially as Old, only three weeks previously, had been battling up into the wind in Wellington and had taken 6 for 54 in 30 overs.

Local radio on the morning of the match, and even up until 9am, reported heavy rain had fallen overnight and more was predicted during the day, and there was little likelihood of a ball being bowled all day. Half an hour later the Auckland Cricket Association was frantically trying to undo the damage made by the announcement. The radio station then tried to reiterate that what it was actually trying to say earlier was that play would start on time at 11am! By 11am a few spots of rain delayed play by half an hour, but it turned out in the end to be a beautiful day.

Despite the discouragement, 15,000 still turned up, but the New Zealand Cricket Council must have lost several thousand pounds on what for them was the equivalent of the Saturday of a Lord's Test.

The pitch had been covered for much of the preceding 24 hours. There was some damp in it, but its reputation for variable bounce later in the game made it advisable to bat first. The ball certainly moved about on the first day with the New Zealand batsmen struggling for lengthy periods of play; however, by the end of the day, they had gathered confidence, admittedly against tired bowlers.

After forty-five minutes of play, John Lever got the ball to swing away from the left-handed John Wright who was caught behind by Taylor for 4.

After lunch, Robert Anderson, a robust operator off the back foot, aimed to hit Ian Botham square and was well caught by Gatting at third slip. Mark Burgess then commanded a stand of 81 with Geoff Howarth and by tea New Zealand's fortunes were looking up.

After the tea interval, play was held up for five minutes as Randall, Botham and Gatting shifted some glinting covers, showing that there was an engaging do-it-yourself informality about Test cricket in New Zealand. In Wellington, one of the New Zealand players had even been helping out serving at one of the tea counters during the tea interval! On resuming, Botham and Randall began cutting off Burgess as he was gathering momentum; he assaulted a half-volley off the back foot and sliced it waist high, well to the left of cover point. It was no catch in ordinary circumstances, but Randall took a couple of quick paces, lifted off and held the catch two-handed, at full stretch. Burgess had fallen for 50. Bev Congdon, who in the match equalled John Reid's record of 58 Test matches, was soon neatly picked up in the gully by Miller off the all-conquering

Botham. John Parker and Geoff Howarth then dug in until the close, New Zealand finishing the day on 162 for 4, Howarth 64 not out. Lever and Botham had done the bulk of the bowling on the first day and, with a little more luck, would have been more suitably rewarded for their 35, admirably sustained overs.

Geoff Howarth, though, had been the star of the day for the home side; he had been expected to be left out of the 12, but ended the day being the batsman to thwart the tourists. When Howarth had come in at 12.15, and for a long time afterwards, it had been hard to envisage him still being there at 6pm and preparing to continue the next morning when the pitch would fare even better for the batsmen. Howarth stuck it out, occasionally driving nicely past mid-off, occasionally hooking. However, he played and missed countless times and when he had made 20 it was clearly England's opinion that he should have been given out, having been caught at the wicket off his glove off an attempted hook at Botham. In his last two hours, however, he played pretty well especially off the front foot wide of mid-on and at the other end there was enough action to keep the big crowd mostly happy.

24,000 packed in to Eden Park for the second day, which turned out to be a boisterous day of cricket, beginning with New Zealand on 162 for 4. John Parker was soon out playing no stroke to Ian Botham, and this brought in the formidable 'Jock' Edwards, 22, who was built like two rugby prop forwards and was currently the most popular cricketer in New Zealand. Against Bob Willis, John Lever and Botham, he produced a respectable defence, and showed himself to be a fine cutter and an enthusiastic hooker from varying parts of the bat. His stand of 96 with Howarth included two extraordinary incidents, the first when he hit Botham over mid-on with Boycott, running back, catching the ball first bounce after it had pitched some feet out of reach. The umpire, unsighted by Boycott, saw the ball in his hand and apparently told Edwards he was out. He started to leave, to the mystification of most of the crowd, but was soon recalled.

By then, without Chris Old (not selected), Geoff Miller (back strain) and Phil Edmonds (bruised shoulder), England's bowling consisted of Botham and Lever, both weary, offering medium-paced long hops and half-volleys respectively. With the score on 242 for 5, Howarth, then 89, hooked at Botham and gave a straightforward catch to Lever on the long-leg boundary, but the chance bounced out of his hands and the batsman ran one. Botham's next ball was similar and Edwards, off a top edge, gave Lever a higher, more awkward catch, exactly what is not wanted by a fielder who has dropped a catch the ball before. This one Lever scarcely touched.

Howarth reached his hundred with two successive straight drives for four off Lever. Edwards then hooked Botham for six to reach 55 out of the partnership of 95 and for a moment England's grip on the innings seemed to be slipping. At this point, however, Edwards missed Lever's slower ball, and after a long wait was adjudged lbw. Richard Hadlee, slashing at Botham, was caught at second slip by Graham Roope, meanwhile Howarth went on and on, and so did Botham and Lever. Eventually, after the two work horses had bowled unchanged for two and a half hours, pausing only for fifteen minutes' rain and a twenty-minute tea interval, Willis replaced Botham. Howarth, cutting at the first ball delivered by Willis, was caught high up at second slip by Roope and the innings rapidly came to an end. New Zealand had scored 315 all out, Howarth had top scored with 122 with Ian Botham taking 5 for 109. The New Zealanders, who at one stage were 35 for 2, had been hauled out of the mire by Howarth whose innings had lasted eight hours and thirty-five minutes. It was Howarth's maiden century and had been a feat of great skill and tenacity. England's openers survived until the close, having scored 30 without loss off seven overs.

The third day saw a day of showers, interruptions and singular inaction, the tide turning slowly but surely in England's direction, in this, the deciding Test. More than an hour of play was lost despite an extra half-hour being added and even that came to a premature close because of bad light. New Zealand completed 47 eight-ball overs before England posted a hundred for the day and this on the best surface on the New Zealand leg of the tour. Derek Randall's path, since his great innings in the Centenary Test, continued to be thorny and his international future was now becoming more doubtful. His departure once again reinforced those doubts. He made a walking shot off Richard Hadlee aiming at wide mid-on and had to go, leg before for 30. His technique was becoming far from perfect and he suffered from his inability to stand still at the crease.

Geoff Boycott was once again dismissed by Richard Collinge, the fast left-arm over the wicket bowler, who equalled Bruce Taylor's New Zealand record of 111 Test wickets. In five innings in the series Collinge had now dismissed Boycott four times. Collinge had found a distinguished rabbit. Boycott was never at his best and took 233 minutes with only four boundaries to reach his fifty. He was barracked although century-maker Geoff Howarth was far slower, which led one former unnamed New Zealand captain to say, 'I long to see him put his left leg down the wicket and go through with his drive. So many half-volleys went unpunished.'

Some of the firmest strokes of the day were made by Clive Radley, playing his best innings in New Zealand, and by the close he had lasted 262 minutes, showing a well organised defence and concentrated discipline with just six boundaries. Graham Roope helped in an unfinished stand of 57, a good base for a substantial lead if England were to assume control. Radley finished on 49, Roope 28 and England on 172 for 2, now having crept to within 143 of New Zealand's 315, with eight wickets still intact.

The fourth day of the deciding Test belonged solely to one man, Clive Radley. It was a triumphant day for the 33-year-old, batting throughout the day and taking his score from his overnight 49 to 154 not out by the close. Radley had been a reluctant choice to replace the injured Mike Brearley in Karachi and had failed to impress the selectors in two trial matches back at home. Tour manager Ken Barrington said, 'We always knew

Clive had endless patience, application and courage.' Radley was still anything but a fast scorer and reached 154 in 616 minutes off 500 balls with 15 boundaries. Starting with 49 overnight he reached his century in 487 minutes, off 397 balls, with ten fours. His third fifty, in partnership with the debonair Ian Botham, came in 107 minutes, his fastest period. But no one had a better technique for the conditions as he walked into his shot or played forward. Radley's innings had been full of gutsy determination and he talked incessantly to himself throughout, urging concentration and driving himself on, though by the end he was near to exhaustion. Radley's innings began with England on 52 for 1 and he was still there at 390 for 5. A magnificent achievement, and all the more credible that he comfortably exceeded the previous highest individual score of the tour, Botham's 126 not out against Canterbury.

The fifth-wicket stand of 97, between solid professional Radley and the young cavalier Botham, provided a startling contrast in styles with Botham hitting 53 off 114 balls, in 133 minutes, before providing Richard Collinge with the wicket-taking record for New Zealand with a snick to wicket-keeper Edwards, thereby beating Bruce Taylor's 111. But Radley's biggest stand was the 139 in 257 minutes with Graham Roope. Roope appeared set for his maiden century until he drove straight to Mark Burgess at mid-on off Stephen Boock for 68. The day belonged to Clive Thornton Radley, who ended on 154, his new partner Bob Taylor on 6 and England 390 for 5, a lead of 75 with two days remaining.

The Test match drifted into a sluggish affair on the fifth day with England adding 39 in two hours from 20.1 eight-ball overs. Their innings of 429 had taken 806 minutes. New Zealand had been partly to blame for the slow over rate with Richard Collinge, the left-arm seamer, taking an age to complete an over, and there were the customary time-wasting antics. At the end, the left-arm spinner Stephen Boock had taken 3 for 2 in his last 19 deliveries and broke a New Zealand wicket aggregate for the season which had stood since back in 1902/03.

Clive Radley was the first wicket to fall in the day when on 158, adding only four to his overnight total; he was caught by John Wright at cover when forcing a back-foot shot off Collinge. Geoff Miller attempted to force Collinge to leg and was out leg before for 15. Phil Edmonds also fell, leg before, to spinner Boock, for 9 when he missed a ball that had floated in. Boock bowled Bob Taylor with a ball that turned sharply from leg and then, finally, John Lever lofted a tame return catch to the same bowler and England were all out for 429, gaining a first-innings lead of 114. Boock ended with impressive figures of 5 for 67, Collinge 4 for 98.

The innings had belonged to Radley, who afterwards said his knock had been masterminded by Geoff Boycott. 'He was like a grand master at chess' said Radley, whose innings of 158 lasted 629 minutes and had seen him face 526 balls. 'At each interval, he sat with me and talked tactics. He insisted on the need for intense concentration and ways to handle each bowler. If I felt down he talked me back into the right mood. Four months ago I couldn't imagine myself playing in a Test, let alone making a century. I do know, however, that I have never been so determined to do the job the skipper wanted.' Boycott, meanwhile, had to have treatment to a scratched cornea from an eye specialist. The condition did not improve, and so it was announced that he was out of the rest of the game. The captaincy was passed on to Bob Willis.

England's poor pre-lunch period was followed by an equally bad afternoon with the unthinkable happening again. In the first innings John Lever dropped two catches, and now it was Phil Edmonds who put down Robert Anderson at square leg. By tea, however, only John Wright had gone with 83 on the board. Wright, trying to play back to Edmonds, saw an outside edge taken behind by Taylor. It was then left to Ian Botham, fielding at backward short leg, who took a superb right-handed catch off the bowling of Geoff Miller to dismiss Anderson for 55.

With two wickets down New Zealand had an arguably frivolous appeal to the umpires about the light; even with two spinners operating, it was upheld. The interruption lasted just eleven minutes. Soon after, Mike Gatting immediately missed catching Geoff Howarth at silly point, but the next delivery flew up off Howarth's pad straight into Gatting's face. Gatting left the field, had some tweezers stuck up his nose to try and straighten it out a bit, and came back on again with it looking slightly bent!

The players soon went off again because of the light, this time for twenty-two minutes. New Zealand ended day five on 112 for 2, two runs behind England and the last day of the series and in fact the tour, was poised to be an interesting one. Could England take the remaining eight wickets and chase down the target set by the New Zealanders?

The final day saw New Zealand dig in. It wasn't long, however, before Mark Burgess fell for 17 when he played back to Phil Edmonds with wicket-keeper Bob Taylor taking the catch. When Bev Congdon was out for 20, playing back to John Lever and snicking a catch to Graham Roope at second slip, New Zealand were beginning to slightly wobble and were now 185 for 4. But it was down to 'Jock' Edwards and that man again, Geoff Howarth, to steady the ship by putting on 87 for the fifth wicket. Edwards though, having just reached his half-century, fell after driving Lever like a bullet straight to Derek Randall, who took the catch at cover point. When Howarth was sixth out, with the score on 287, the home side had saved the Test. Howarth fell having just scored his second century of the game, when on 102, he mis-pulled Geoff Miller and was bowled. It had been a heroic effort by the right-hander. Miller then bowled Richard Hadlee when he attempted to cut a low ball and then, with the score on 350, the eighth wicket fell when Lance Cairns was plumb lbw to Phil Edmonds. Finally, when the score had reached 382 for 8, the captains shook hands and the Test ended in a draw with the series ending all square.

It was very much out of character for an England side to have made a less positive effort to win a Test. They had bowled New Zealand out in their first innings for 315 by ten past five on the second day. England then took until just before lunch on the fifth day (it was a six-day match) to score 429! This had enabled New Zealand to escape comfortably in the end with a draw. Bob Willis was relieved to have finished the Test so he could go and watch his hero, Bob Dylan, perform in concert at Western Springs. For Willis it had been a terribly boring game on a very flat wicket; he had even employed his spinners Edmonds and Miller to make the game more interesting. Willis, like the rest of the tour party, just wanted to get home.

Geoff Boycott, despising sham modesty and pretence, bluntly declared at the end of the drawn Test that he wanted to continue as England captain. The self-confessed practical Yorkshire man, who took over when Mike Brearley broke his arm in Karachi, clearly saw himself as the leader the following season when Pakistan and New Zealand shared six Tests in England – and beyond that, the defence of the Ashes in Australia the following winter.

Boycott stated he was pleased tactically with the way his captaincy had developed and that Ian Botham and Phil Edmonds had represented the great plusses of the tour. He also felt that the apprentices, Mike Gatting and Paul Downton, had learnt a lot, but that the eternal headache of the middle-order batting remained uncured. Boycott had thought the pitches in New Zealand caused a problem (apart from Christchurch and Auckland), helping seam bowling to an inordinate degree and that no batsman had felt in form until Christchurch because of the pitches.

Bob Willis was astonished at the length of Geoff Boycott's umpire reports in New Zealand which would run to three foolscap pages. The reports would state everything from the time of day that leg before decisions were turned down to leg byes that were not signalled.

So England's long winter tour had finally come to an end with both Test series having been, fairly, drawn. The tour had provided mixed success and England would return home slightly disappointed to have not won the series in New Zealand.

Thoughts now, however, would turn to the forthcoming return fixtures in England against the same opponents and the build-up to the next winter's Ashes down under. Boycott's captaincy dreams did not materialise as Mike Brearley returned to lead a triumphant England in the summer of '78.

What followed …

The three-Test series in 1978 against Pakistan was dominated on the whole by England, winning the first two Tests at Edgbaston and Lord's by an innings. The third Test was drawn. The first Test at Edgbaston saw Chris Old destroy Pakistan with 7 for 50 before centuries from Clive Radley and Ian Botham gave England a first-innings lead of 288. Pakistan had been bowled out for 231 mainly by the spin of Phil Edmonds and Geoff Miller to give England victory by an innings and 57 runs. At Lord's it was another century by Ian Botham that gave England a healthy first-innings score of 364 before bowling out Pakistan twice for 105 and 139 to win by an innings and 120 runs. Bob Willis took 5 for 47 and Edmonds 4 for 6 off eight overs in the first innings with Botham ripping through Pakistan in the second, taking 8 for 34. The rain-affected third Test at Headingley was drawn, giving England the series 2-0.

England saw New Zealand arrive for the second half of the summer and continued where they had left off against Pakistan, in convincing style, crushing the Kiwis 3-0. In the first Test at The Oval, England won by seven wickets with David Gower winning man of the match for his 111. The second Test at Trent Bridge was won by an innings and 119 runs, mainly due to Geoff Boycott's 131 and man of the match Ian Botham's 6 for 34 and 3 for 59. England's fine summer ended with another win, by seven wickets, at Lord's with Botham once again the star, taking 6 for 101 and 5 for 39. Man of the match, however, went to New Zealand's Geoff Howarth who hit 123 in the first innings. The New Zealanders were routed for 67 in their second innings. A hugely satisfying summer for England and now all eyes were focused on retaining the Ashes.

Mike Brearley led England to an historic 5-1 win in Australia, winning the Tests in Brisbane, Perth, Sydney (twice) and Adelaide. Their only defeat came in the third Test at the MCG in Melbourne. England had been pretty dominant in all areas. The series, however, was often overshadowed by Kerry Packer's second season of World Series Cricket.

The Australians were handicapped more than England due to the loss of a wealth of players lured away by Packer's World Series initiative. Australian fast bowler Rodney Hogg came to prominence, taking 41 wickets in the series at an average of 12.85.

England had been basically just too strong for Australia. They won the first Test at Brisbane by seven wickets, with Derek Randall (74 not out) and 21-year-old David Gower (48 not out) seeing England to their target of 170. Gower's century in the second Test at Perth helped England to a 166-run victory and a 2-0 series lead. The Australians were given some hope following victory in the third Test, thanks to Graeme Wood's century and ten wickets for Hogg. But comprehensive victories at Sydney (twice) and Adelaide saw England romp to a series win.

By now, the Australian Cricket Board was suffering financially. Trying to take on Kerry Packer was becoming a no-win situation. Packer gave the impression that there was no end to the amount of money he was prepared to invest in World Series Cricket.

The only way forward for the Australian Cricket Board was to hold meetings with the World Series Cricket organisation and endeavour to resolve all the outstanding issues. At the time though, Packer himself was also keen to find a solution. He did not have as much money left as was thought. So in March 1979 it was Packer who went about setting up the meetings with the ACB chairman, Bob Parish, to seek an agreement in the best interests of Australian cricket. On 30 May 1979, Parish surprised and shocked many with a statement that Kerry Packer's Channel Nine Network had won exclusive rights to televise Australian cricket and that it had been granted a ten-year contract to promote and market the game through a new company, PBL Marketing.

The legacy World Series Cricket left, especially for one-day international cricket, was huge. Night cricket under floodlights and coloured clothing would soon become the norm. At the time of the discussions the Australian World Series cricketers were on tour in the Caribbean and had no input into the negotiations. Some of the players were left disillusioned and apprehensive that they might suffer in the future from the ACB. None of Packer's contracted players were selected for the tours of England and India and missed out on playing in the 1979 World Cup.

That year's *Wisden* commented that when the Australian Board first found Packer at their throats, the rest of the cricket world supported them to the hilt and now, when it suited Australia, they had brushed their friends aside to meet their own ends.

The following winter in 1979/80 Greg Chappell was restored as Australian captain and the team contained an even mixture of World Series Cricket and non-World Series Cricket players and the format of the triangular one-day tournament was played just like the previous season of World Series Cricket had been. The format received heavy criticism, but it made a healthy profit, with much of it going to Packer's PBL Marketing as opposed to the Australian Cricket Board.

Another chapter in the history of the great game of cricket had only just begun.

Appendix A:

The tour results in Pakistan and New Zealand

THE TOUR RESULTS IN PAKISTAN

TOUR MATCH 1 at the Pindi Club Ground, Rawalpindi, 30 November, 1 and 2 December 1977

BCCP PATRON'S XI V ENGLAND XI

BCCP PATRON'S XI: S. Ahmed, M. Nazar, H. Rashid, J. Miandad, S. Altaf, W. Raja, M. Khan, A. Qadir, W. Bari (Captain & w/k), I. Qasim and L. Ali

ENGLAND XI: M. Brearley (Captain), G. Boycott, B. Rose, D. Randall, G. Roope, C. Old, G. Miller, R. Taylor (w/k), P. Edmonds, R. Willis and M. Hendrick

BCCP Patron's XI: 151 (48.3 overs) (S. Ahmed 52, G. Miller 6 for 62) & 118 for 6 declared (41 overs)

England XI: 64 for 9 declared (44 overs) (L. Ali 5 for 23) & 32 for 1 (18 overs)

MATCH DRAWN

England won the toss and decided to field

TOUR MATCH 2 at the Iqbal Stadium, Faisalabad, 4, 5 and 6 December

UNITED BANK XI V ENGLAND XI

UNITED BANK XI: T. Ali, S. Mohammad, H. Rashid, K. Irtiza, N. Valika (Captain), M. Akhtar, Arifuddin (w/k), A. Hameed, N. Ahmed, S. Pervez and S. Bakht

ENGLAND XI: M. Brearley (Captain), G. Boycott, B. Rose, D. Randall, G. Roope, M. Gatting, I. Botham, G. Cope, P. Edmonds, P. Downton (w/k) and M. Hendrick

United Bank XI: 210 for 4 declared (64.7 overs) (Sadiq Mohammad 53, Nasir Valika 53 not out) & 58 for 2 (23 overs)

England XI: 284 for 1 declared (73 overs) (G. Boycott 123 not out, B. Rose 110 not out) & 165 for 3 declared (38.1 overs) (G. Roope 102 not out)

MATCH DRAWN

England won the toss and decided to bat

TOUR MATCH 3 at the Services Ground, Peshawar, 8, 9 and 10 December

NORTH WEST FRONTIER PROVINCE GOVERNOR'S XI V ENGLAND XI

GOVERNOR'S XI: A. Zahid, A. Pervez, S. Ahmed, T. Arif (w/k), A. Rana, P. Mir, W. Raja (Captain), H. Jamil, A. Raqib, Ehteshamuddin and F. Zaman

ENGLAND XI: M. Brearley (Captain), G. Boycott, B. Rose, D. Randall, G. Roope, G. Miller, I. Botham, C. Old, R. Taylor (w/k), J. Lever and R. Willis

England XI: 285 for 3 declared (76 overs) (G. Boycott 115 not out, G. Roope 63 not out, M. Brearley 57) & 122 for 3 declared (31.4 overs) (D. Randall 57)

Governor's XI: 127 (39.4 overs) (J. Lever 3 for 49, C. Old 3 for 11) & 68 (28.3 overs) (J. Lever 3 for 11).

ENGLAND XI won by 212 runs

TOUR MATCH 4 at the Gaddafi Stadium, Lahore, 14, 15, 16, 18 and 19 December

First Test – PAKISTAN v ENGLAND

PAKISTAN: Mudassar Nazar, Sadiq Mohammad, Shafiq Ahmed, Haroon Rashid, Javed Miandad, Wasim Raja, Abdul Qadir, Wasim Bari (Captain & w/k), Sarfraz Nawaz, Iqbal Qasim and Liaqat Ali

ENGLAND: Mike Brearley (Captain), Geoff Boycott, Brian Rose, Derek Randall, Graham Roope, Geoff Miller, Chris Old, Bob Taylor (w/k), Geoff Cope, John Lever and Bob Willis

Pakistan: 407 for 9 declared (133 overs) (H. Rashid 122, M. Nazar 122, J. Miandad 71, G. Miller 3 for 102, G. Cope 3 for 102) and 106 for 3 (28 overs)

England: 288 (135.7 overs) (G. Miller 98 not out, G. Boycott 63, S. Nawaz 4 for 68, I. Qasim 3 for 57)

MATCH DRAWN

Pakistan won the toss and decided to bat

Test Debuts: PAKISTAN – Abdul Qadir. ENGLAND – Brian Rose and Geoff Cope

TOUR MATCH 5 at the Zafar Ali Stadium, Sahiwal, 23 December

First One-Day International – PAKISTAN v ENGLAND

35 overs – 8 ball overs

PAKISTAN: Mudassar Nazar, Sadiq Mohammad, Shafiq Ahmed, Javed Miandad, Wasim Raja, Parvez Mir, Hasan Jamil, Wasim Bari (Captain & w/k), Saleem Altaf, Aamer Hameed and Liaqat Ali

ENGLAND: Mike Brearley (Captain), Brian Rose, Mike Gatting, Derek Randall, Chris Old, Graham Roope, Ian Botham, Phil Edmonds, Geoff Miller, Paul Downton (w/k) and Mike Hendrick

Pakistan: 208 for 6 (35 overs) (J. Miandad 77 not out, I. Botham 3 for 39)

England: 212 for 7 (35 overs) (B. Rose 54)

ENGLAND WON BY 3 WICKETS

Pakistan won the toss and decided to bat

ODI Debuts: PAKISTAN – Mudassar Nazar, Shafiq Ahmed, Hasan Jamil, Aamer Hameed and Liaqat Ali. ENGLAND – Brian Rose, Mike Gatting, Phil Edmonds and Paul Downton.

TOUR MATCH 6 at the Gaddafi Stadium, Lahore on 26, 27 and 28 December

HABIB BANK XI v ENGLAND XI

No toss made

Match Abandoned

TOUR MATCH 7 at the Gaddafi Stadium, Lahore on 28 December

HABIB BANK XI v ENGLAND XI

30 overs – 8 ball overs

HABIB BANK XI: T. Ali, A. Pervez, M. Akhtar, J. Miandad (Captain), A. Khan, R. Israr, J. Hussain, W. Mirza, H. Jamil, A. Raqib and M. Iqbal (w/k)

ENGLAND XI: Mike Brearley (Captain), Geoff Boycott, Brian Rose, Derek Randall, Graham Roope, Ian Botham, Bob Taylor (w/k), Phil Edmonds, John Lever, Geoff Cope and Bob Willis

England: 166 for 7 (30 overs) (G. Boycott 56, D. Randall 49)

Habib Bank XI: 103 for 7 (30 overs)

ENGLAND WON BY 63 RUNS

Habib Bank XI won the toss and elected to field

TOUR MATCH 8 at the Jinnah Stadium, Sialkot, 30 December
Second One-Day International – PAKISTAN v ENGLAND
35 overs – 8 ball overs

PAKISTAN: Mudassar Nazar, Sadiq Mohammad, Shafiq Ahmed, Haroon Rashid, Javed Miandad, Wasim Raja, Wasim Bari (Captain & w/k), Hasan Jamil, Saleem Altaf, Iqbal Qasim and Sikander Bakht

ENGLAND: Brian Rose, Graham Roope, Geoff Miller, Derek Randall, Mike Gatting, Ian Botham, Geoff Boycott (Captain), Bob Taylor (w/k), Phil Edmonds, John Lever and Geoff Cope

Pakistan: 151 all out (33.7 overs) (J. Lever 3 for 18)

England: 152 for 4 (32.7 overs) (D. Randall 51 not out)

ENGLAND WON BY 6 WICKETS

England won the toss and decided to field

ODI Debuts: PAKISTAN – Haroon Rashid, Iqbal Qasim and Sikander Bakht. ENGLAND – Geoff Cope

TOUR MATCH 9 at the Niaz Stadium, Hyderabad, 2, 3, 4, 6 and 7 January 1978
Second Test Match – PAKISTAN v ENGLAND

PAKISTAN: Mudassar Nazar, Sadiq Mohammad, Shafiq Ahmed, Haroon Rashid, Javed Miandad, Wasim Raja, Abdul Qadir, Wasim Bari (Captain & w/k), Iqbal Qasim, Liaqat Ali and Sikander Bakht

ENGLAND: Geoff Boycott, Mike Brearley (Captain), Brian Rose, Derek Randall, Graham Roope, Geoff Miller, Bob Taylor (w/k), Phil Edmonds, Geoff Cope, John Lever and Bob Willis

Pakistan: 275 all out (79.6 overs) (H. Rashid 108, J. Miandad 88 not out, P. Edmonds 3 for 75) & 259 for 4 declared (88 overs) (M. Nazar 66, J. Miandad 61 not out)

England: 191 all out (86.6 overs) (G. Boycott 79, A. Qadir 6 for 44) and 186 for 1 (84.1 overs) (G. Boycott 100 not out, M. Brearley 74)

MATCH DRAWN

Pakistan won the toss and decided to bat

TOUR MATCH 10 at the Bahawal Stadium, Bahawalpur on 9, 10 and 11 January

PUNJAB XI v ENGLAND XI

PUNJAB XI: M. Khan, S. Ali, A. Zia, N. Valika, W. Raja (Capt), A. Rana, A. Ali (w/k), F. Shera, N. Ahmed, M. Khan and J. Hussain

ENGLAND XI: Brian Rose, Derek Randall, Graham Roope, Geoff Miller, Mike Brearley (Captain), Chris Old, Mike Gatting, Ian Botham, Phil Edmonds, Paul Downton (w/k) and Mike Hendrick

Punjab XI: 217 for 9 declared (67 overs) (M. Khan 97 not out, G. Miller 4 for 52) and 193 for 9 (38 overs) (W. Raja 49, P. Edmonds 3 for 50)

England: 334 for 5 declared (99.4 overs) (D. Randall 87, G. Roope 85, B. Rose 72)

MATCH DRAWN

Punjab XI won the toss and decided to bat

TOUR MATCH 11 at the Gaddafi Stadium, Lahore, 13 January

Third One-Day International – PAKISTAN v ENGLAND

35 overs – 8 ball overs

PAKISTAN: Mudassar Nazar, Arshad Pervez, Shafiq Ahmed, Javed Miandad, Wasim Raja, Mohsin Khan, Hasan Jamil, Sarfraz Nawaz, Wasim Bari (Captain & w/k), Aamer Hameed and Iqbal Qasim

ENGLAND: Geoff Boycott, Mike Brearley (Captain), Derek Randall, Mike Gatting, Ian Botham, Chris Old, Graham Roope, Bob Taylor (w/k), Phil Edmonds, John Lever and Geoff Cope

Pakistan: 158 for 6 (35 overs) (M. Khan 51 not out)

England: 122 all out (31.6 overs) (W. Raja 3 for 23)

PAKISTAN WON BY 36 RUNS

England won the toss and decided to field

ODI Debuts: PAKISTAN – Aarshad Pervez

TOUR MATCH 12 at the National Stadium, Karachi on 15 January

SIND XI v ENGLAND XI

35 overs – 8 ball overs

SIND XI: W. Mirza, M. Akhtar, M. Khan, N. Valika, I. Faqih, A. Sanjrani, S. Israr (w/k), A. Khan, N. Ahmed, S. Iqbal and S. Bakht

ENGLAND XI: Mike Brearley (Captain), Geoff Boycott, Brian Rose, Geoff Miller, Mike Gatting, Ian Botham, Phil Edmonds, Paul Downton (w/k), John Lever, Bob Willis and Mike Hendrick

England: 141 for 5 (35 overs) (M. Gatting 59)

Sind XI: 142 for 7 (33.4 overs) (M. Khan 59, R. Willis 4 for 17)

SIND XI WON BY 3 WICKETS

TOUR MATCH 13 at the National Stadium, Karachi, 18, 19, 20, 22 and 23 January

Third Test Match – PAKISTAN v ENGLAND

PAKISTAN: Mudassar Nazar, Shafiq Ahmed, Mohsin Khan, Haroon Rashid, Javed Miandad, Wasim Raja, Abdul Qadir, Wasim Bari (Captain & w/k), Sarfraz Nawaz, Iqbal Qasim and Sikander Bakht

ENGLAND: Geoff Boycott (Captain), Brian Rose, Derek Randall, Graham Roope, Mike Gatting, Geoff Miller, Bob Taylor (w/k), Phil Edmonds, Geoff Cope, John Lever and Bob Willis

England: 266 all out (123.1 overs) (G. Roope 56, A. Qadir 4 for 81, I. Qasim 3 for 56) and 222 for 5 (89 overs) (G. Boycott 56, D. Randall 55)

Pakistan: 281 all out (95 overs) (M. Nazar 76, P. Edmonds 7 for 66)

MATCH DRAWN

England won the toss and decided to bat

Debuts: PAKISTAN – Mohsin Khan. ENGLAND – Mike Gatting

THE TEST SERIES WAS DRAWN 0-0

Geoff Boycott had excelled in the three Tests against Pakistan and headed the batting averages for England for the series with an average of 82.25. Boycott scored 329 runs in his five innings. Second, surprisingly, was Geoff Miller (mainly thanks to his 98 not out in Lahore) who had scored 117 runs from his four innings which had resulted in an average of 39.00. All-in-all England, apart from Boycott, had not performed that well with the bat!

Three Pakistan players averaged above 50. Javed Miandad had hit 262 runs from five innings to finish with an average of 131.00, Haroon Rashid (337 from five) finished with 84.25 and Mudassar Nazar, 309 from five innings, finished with an average of 61.80.

As far as the bowling averages went it was Phil Edmonds who topped the list for England with ten wickets and an average of 23.60 followed by big Bob Willis whose seven wickets had produced an average of 27.14. Edmonds of course had shot to the top of the list with his 7 for 66 in the last Test in Karachi.

Three Pakistani spinners topped their bowling averages, Wasim Raja with an average of 22.66 (although he only took three wickets), followed by the leading wicket-taker Abdul Qadir, who took 12 at an average of 25.41, and Iqbal Qasim who took ten wickets at 26.00.

THE TOUR RESULTS IN NEW ZEALAND

TOUR MATCH 1 at Eden Park, Auckland, 27, 28 and 29 January

AUCKLAND v ENGLAND XI

AUCKLAND: P. Webb, R. Kasper, J. Wiltshire, M. Burgess, G. Vivian (Captain), J. Reid (w/k), R. Arblaster, J. McIntyre, L. Stott, M. Snedden and J. Cushen

ENGLAND XI: Geoff Boycott (Captain), Brian Rose, Clive Radley, Mike Gatting, Graham Roope, Geoff Miller, Ian Botham, Bob Taylor (w/k), Chris Old, Phil Edmonds and Mike Hendrick

England: 210 all out (69.2 overs) (M. Snedden 3 for 35, J. Cushen 3 for 72) and 208 for 3 declared (62.1 overs) (B. Rose 107)

Auckland: 182 for 4 declared (54 overs) (M. Burgess 74 not out) and 114 for 3 (39 overs) (R. Kasper 61 not out)

MATCH DRAWN

Auckland won the toss and decided to field

TOUR MATCH 2 at Seddon Park, Hamilton, 30 January

NORTHERN DISTRICTS v ENGLAND XI

One-Day Match – 35 Eight-ball overs

NORTHERN DISTRICTS: J. Wright, J. Gibson, G. Howarth, J. Parker (Captain), A. Roberts, B. Dunning, M. Wright (w/k), K. Puna, C. Dickeson, R. Collinge and P. Anderson

ENGLAND XI: Graham Roope, Brian Rose, Mike Gatting, Derek Randall, Ian Botham, Geoff Miller, Phil Edmonds, John Lever, Geoff Cope, Paul Downton (w/k) and Bob Willis (Captain)

England: 164 for 9 (35 overs) (C. Dickeson 3 for 58)

Northern Districts: 83 for 3 (20.3 overs)

ENGLAND WON BY 14 RUNS ON A FASTER SCORING RATE

When play was halted at 5.08pm, Northern Districts needed to have scored 97 to win

Northern Districts won the toss and decided to field

TOUR MATCH 3 at Pukekura Park, New Plymouth, 1, 2 and 3 February

CENTRAL DISTRICTS v ENGLAND XI

CENTRAL DISTRICTS: I. Rutherford, R. Anderson, M. Shrimpton (Captain), M. Toynbee, G. Edwards, T. Horne, I. Smith (w/k), D. Bracewell, D. O'Sullivan, D. Aberhart and A. Jordan

ENGLAND XI: Brian Rose, Clive Radley, Derek Randall, Graham Roope, Mike Gatting, Geoff Miller, Chris Old, Geoff Cope, Paul Downton (w/k), John Lever and Bob Willis (Captain)

England: 296 for 6 declared (74.1 overs) (M. Gatting 66, G. Roope 55, C. Old 55, A. Jordan 3 for 38) and 104 all out (49.1 overs) (D. O'Sullivan 5 for 14, D. Aberhart 3 for 33)

Central Districts: 198 all out (52.5 overs) (R. Willis 3 for 45, G. Miller 3 for 56) and 202 all out (43 overs)

MATCH TIED

England won the toss and decided to bat

TOUR MATCH 4 at Lancaster Park, Christchurch, 5, 6 and 7 February

CANTERBURY v ENGLAND XI

CANTERBURY: P. Coman, B. Hadlee, N. Parker, P. McEwan, B. Congdon (Captain), D. Stead, M. Ryan (w/k), R. Hadlee, D. Hadlee, W. Eddington and S. Boock

ENGLAND XI: Geoff Boycott (Captain), Geoff Miller, Derek Randall, Clive Radley, Mike Gatting, Ian Botham, Bob Taylor (w/k), Chris Old, Phil Edmonds, Mike Hendrick and Bob Willis

England: 173 all out (75 overs) (C. Old 51, R. Hadlee 5 for 50) and 230 for 4 declared (55 overs) (I. Botham 126 not out)

Canterbury: 144 all out (41.3 overs) (P. Coman 51, R. Willis 4 for 46, I. Botham 3 for 28) and 142 for 5 (44 overs) (R. Hadlee 56)

MATCH DRAWN

Canterbury won the toss and decided to field

TOUR MATCH 5 at the Basin Reserve, Wellington, 10, 11, 12, 14 and 15 February

NEW ZEALAND v ENGLAND – FIRST TEST

NEW ZEALAND: John Wright, Robert Anderson, Geoff Howarth, Mark Burgess (Captain), Bev Congdon, John Parker, Warren Lees (w/k), Richard Hadlee, Dayle Hadlee, Richard Collinge and Stephen Boock

ENGLAND: Brian Rose, Geoff Boycott (Captain), Geoff Miller, Bob Taylor (w/k), Derek Randall, Graham Roope, Ian Botham, Chris Old, Mike Hendrick, Phil Edmonds and Bob Willis

New Zealand: 228 all out (87.6 overs) (J. Wright 55, C. Old 6 for 54) and 123 all out (44.3 overs) (R. Willis 5 for 32)

England: 215 all out (94.4 overs) (G. Boycott 77, R. Hadlee 4 for 74) and 64 all out (27.3 overs) (R. Hadlee 6 for 26, R. Collinge 3 for 35)

NEW ZEALAND WON BY 72 RUNS

England won the toss and decided to field

Debuts: New Zealand – John Wright and Stephen Boock

TOUR MATCH 6 at Carisbrook, Dunedin, 17, 18 and 19 February

OTAGO v ENGLAND XI

OTAGO: W. Blair, S. McCullum, B. McKechnie, K. Campbell, P. Facoory, W. Lees (Captain & w/k), B. Blair, L. Cairns, C. Kirk, G. Thomson and P. Petherick

ENGLAND XI: Derek Randall, Geoff Boycott (Captain), Graham Roope, Clive Radley, Mike Gatting, Ian Botham, Phil Edmonds, John Lever, Geoff Cope, Mike Hendrick and Paul Downton (w/k)

Otago: 130 all out (47.3 overs) (J. Lever 5 for 59, I. Botham 3 for 33) and 146 all out (47.4 overs) (I. Botham 7 for 58)

England: 195 all out (102 overs) (L. Cairns 4 for 73, B. McKechnie 3 for 46) and 82 for 4 (23.6 overs) (G. Thomson 3 for 44)

ENGLAND XI WON BY 6 WICKETS

Otago won the toss and decided to field

TOUR MATCH 7 at Temuka Oval, Temuka, 20, 21 and 22 February

YOUNG NEW ZEALAND v ENGLAND XI

YOUNG NEW ZEALAND: I. Rutherford, B. Edgar (Captain), J. Coney, J. Reid, G. Edwards (w/k), B. Blair, B. McKechnie, D. Bracewell, E. Gray, M. Snedden and B. Bracewell

ENGLAND XI: Geoff Boycott (Captain), Brian Rose, Derek Randall, Clive Radley, Graham Roope, Geoff Miller, Bob Taylor (w/k), Chris Old, Phil Edmonds, John Lever and Bob Willis

England: 310 all out (114.7 overs) (D. Randall 104, E. Gray 4 for 58, D. Bracewell 4 for 87)

Young New Zealand: 139 all out (57.1 overs) (G. Miller 6 for 71) and 148 all out (50.4 overs) (J. Lever 4 for 26, G. Miller 4 for 53)

ENGLAND XI WON BY AN INNINGS AND 23 RUNS

England XI won the toss and decided to bat

TOUR MATCH 8 at Lancaster Park, Christchurch, 24, 25, 26, 28 February and 1 March

NEW ZEALAND v ENGLAND – SECOND TEST

NEW ZEALAND: John Wright, Robert Anderson, Geoff Howarth, Mark Burgess (Captain), Bev Congdon, John Parker, Warren Lees (w/k), Richard Hadlee, Richard Collinge, Stephen Boock and Ewen Chatfield

ENGLAND: Brian Rose, Geoff Boycott (Captain), Derek Randall, Graham Roope, Geoff Miller, Clive Radley, Ian Botham, Bob Taylor (w/k), Chris Old, Phil Edmonds and Bob Willis

England: 418 all out (145.5 overs) (I. Botham 103, G. Miller 89, G. Roope 50, P. Edmonds 50, G. Boycott 77, R. Hadlee 4 for 147, R. Collinge 3 for 89) and 96 for 4 declared (22 overs)

New Zealand: 235 all out (92.7 overs) (R. Anderson 62, J. Parker 53 not out, I. Botham 5 for 73, P. Edmonds 4 for 38) and 105 all out (27 overs) (R. Willis 4 for 14, I. Botham 3 for 38)

ENGLAND WON BY 174 RUNS

England won the toss and decided to bat

Debut: England – Clive Radley

TOUR MATCH 9 at Eden Park, Auckland, 4, 5, 6, 8, 9 and 10 March

NEW ZEALAND v ENGLAND – THIRD TEST

NEW ZEALAND: John Wright, Robert Anderson, Geoff Howarth, Mark Burgess (Captain), Bev Congdon, John Parker, Graham 'Jock' Edwards (w/k), Richard Hadlee, Lance Cairns, Richard Collinge and Stephen Boock

ENGLAND: Geoff Boycott (Captain), Derek Randall, Clive Radley, Graham Roope, Mike Gatting, Ian Botham, Bob Taylor (w/k), Geoff Miller, Phil Edmonds, John Lever and Bob Willis

New Zealand: 315 all out (105.6 overs) (G. Howarth 122, G. Edwards 55, M. Burgess 50, I. Botham 5 for 109, J. Lever 3 for 96) and 382 for 8 (118 overs) (G. Howarth 102, R. Anderson 55, G. Edwards 54, G. Miller 3 for 99, P. Edmonds 3 for 107)

England: 429 all out (156.3 overs) (C. Radley 158, G. Roope 68, G. Boycott 54, I. Botham 53, S. Boock 5 for 67, R. Collinge 4 for 98)

MATCH DRAWN

New Zealand won the toss and decided to bat

THE TEST SERIES WAS DRAWN 1-1

Topping England's batting averages for the Test series in New Zealand was Clive Radley who had scored 173 runs from his two innings (thanks to his top score of 158 in the last Test at Auckland) with an average of 86.50. New Zealand's batting averages were headed by 'Jock' Edwards with an average of 54.50 (109 runs from two innings) followed by Geoff Howarth's average of 44.00 (264 runs from six innings).

England's bowling averages were topped by Bob Willis at 18.21 (14 wickets) followed closely by Ian Botham's 18.29 (17 wickets). Botham was leading wicket-taker in the three-match series.

Spinner Stephen Boock headed the New Zealand bowling averages with 18.42 (7 wickets) followed by Richard Collinge's 19.35 (15 wickets).

Appendix B:

The following questions were asked to Mike Brearley, Bob Willis and Bob Taylor about the tour, between February 2011 and November 2015

Author to MIKE BREARLEY: The tour to Pakistan was certainly an interesting one to say the least! The third match was in Peshawar against the West Frontier Province Governor's XI on a ground on which you had hit 312, your highest first-class score, back in 1965 for the MCC Under-25 side against North Zone. Do you have any memories of that innings?

MIKE BREARLEY: Yes, several. I remember having a hit after 100, and suddenly realising I might score 200, so I applied myself again, and the same again after I got to 200!

Author to BOB TAYLOR: It must have been nice, due to Alan Knott's involvement with Packer, going on an overseas tour as now the side's number one wicket-keeper?

BOB TAYLOR: Yes, I had almost resigned myself to the solitary Test match debut in Christchurch on the 70/71 tour, knowing that unless Alan Knott had a dramatic drop in form, I would never be able to take his place.

Author to BOB TAYLOR: After defeating the North West Frontier Province Governor's XI in Peshawar, prior to the first Test, can you remember attending that night, a performance of *Romeo and Juliet* by the London Shakespeare Group?

BOB TAYLOR: Yes, very well, because although apart from the England touring team, the audience were mostly Muslim students and probably fairly westernised, when Romeo embraced Juliet (they weren't allowed to kiss in public) all the locals started to cheer and laugh.

Author to BOB TAYLOR: What was it like in the first Test in Lahore witnessing from behind the stumps – still on record – the slowest Test century of all time by Mudassar Nazar?

BOB TAYLOR: Very boring, it ended up being a two-innings five-day Test, and it was the longest time I've ever spent in the field. We came off the field in the Pakistan innings just after tea on the third day!

BOB WILLIS meanwhile remembered the innings as 'Boring beyond belief' and *MIKE BREARLEY* stated 'Not much. Only that it was slow.'

Author to BOB WILLIS: That first Test saw regular rioting by the home crowd. How frightening was it to play in front of such a hostile crowd? Do you have any amusing stories about what went on?

BOB WILLIS: It was not particularly unsettling. Mike Brearley said if there was any trouble all congregate in the middle of the square. As soon as the riot broke out he sprinted off the field!!!

MIKE BREARLEY: It was frightening. But the crowd were very kind, coming up to us and saying 'We are not angry you. Police behaviour very bad.'

BOB TAYLOR: I cannot remember anything particularly amusing in Pakistan, especially when the police and army were firing tear gas at the rioting crowd! From memory I think Mr Bhutto had been arrested and Benazir Bhutto and her mother were trying to hold illegal meetings on the Lahore cricket ground during the Test.

Author to BOB TAYLOR: Did you find keeping in the Test matches in Pakistan a challenge?

BOB TAYLOR: It's probably the most difficult part of the World to keep wicket, simply because no matter who is bowling, the ball hardly ever beats the bat. CONCENTRATION is paramount for a keeper and on a long hot day you hardly touch the ball except for throw-ins from the fielders, but in the final over after a long sticky day, a batsman can nick one or run down the wicket to create a possible stumping chance. That's what wicket-keeping is all about.

Author to BOB WILLIS: Did you find bowling in those Test matches in Pakistan a challenge?

BOB WILLIS: Yes. The dead pitches offered nothing to any bowlers.

Author to MIKE BREARLEY: You had your arm broken by Sikander Bakht in Karachi against the Sind XI. You had your arm set in plaster at the hospital in Karachi. What memories do you have of the event?

MIKE BREARLEY: Yes – it was very painful. The hospital was fine and they were very kind.

Author to BOB WILLIS: It must have been a relief to get to New Zealand for that leg of the tour?

BOB WILLIS: It sure was. Clean fresh air, wonderful food and wine. We thought we had arrived in paradise.

BOB TAYLOR: It was, from the time we got off a PIA flight in Singapore and boarded an Air New Zealand flight to Auckland. I remember Mike Hendrick, my Derbyshire colleague, saying that his highlight of the whole tour was now being in New Zealand and being able to have a SOLID S**T!!

Author to BOB WILLIS: The three-day game against Central Districts in New Plymouth, in which you captained the team, was to have an exciting finish. The match was tied and you took the final wicket. Can you remember anything about the end of this game?

BOB WILLIS: Yes, it was a make or break situation and obviously I did not want to lose my first match in charge.

Author to BOB TAYLOR: Unfortunately for England and yourself, you played in the first Test, at the Basin Reserve in Wellington, in which New Zealand defeated England for the very first time in a Test. After bowling New Zealand out for 123 in their second innings you must have put your feet up thinking job done and the batsmen would easily knock off the 137 to win (but you were bowled out for 64!). Do you recall any memories of that Test?

BOB TAYLOR: Just batting badly, from Geoff Boycott our captain bowled round his legs by Richie Collinge (left-armer) and unfortunately a young schoolboy asking Geoff for his autograph as he walked off the field; he refused quite bluntly making the young boy cry, our physio Bernie Thomas eventually getting Boycs to apologise and sign his autograph book. It was also very windy. Bob Willis's first ball of the match getting John Wright to nick his first ball in Test cricket and not being given out, going on to get a good score.

Author to BOB WILLIS: You had more success as a bowler in the Tests in New Zealand. You must have been well cheesed off though, in losing the Test at the Basin Reserve?

BOB WILLIS: Very. Yes, it was a shocking pitch, but we should have made the runs. Not England's strongest batting line-up however.

Author to MIKE BREARLEY: I understand you rejoined the tour in New Zealand?

MIKE BREARLEY: I did not rejoin the tour. I came to New Zealand for three weeks or less to write some articles for a newspaper. I arrived just after the Wellington Test had finished.

Author to MIKE BREARLEY: How long did it take for the break in your arm to heal and when did you return to playing?

MIKE BREARLEY: I resumed playing in April of that year – too soon, I'm afraid. I don't think it fully healed until after that season in the UK.

Author to BOB TAYLOR: Any other comments about the tour in general?

BOB TAYLOR: As ever the New Zealand hospitality was first class, a wonderful country, and very sad today to see Christchurch in the mess it's in. I made my debut in Christchurch and for a professional sportsman to represent your country for the first time is the pinnacle.

(Taylor is referring to the earthquake of a magnitude of 6.3 that hit Christchurch on 22 February 2011 that caused widespread damage throughout the city.)

Appendix C:

Interview With Mark Burgess

MARK Burgess was captain of New Zealand for the visit of the touring England side in 1978. In the following interview, Mark not only recalls the Test series, which included New Zealand's historic first ever Test win over England at the Basin Reserve, but also other events in his career as well.

Burgess was a right-hand batsman who bowled right-arm off-breaks and who captained New Zealand between 1978 and 1980. He played 50 Tests and 26 one-day internationals. His highest Test score was 119 not out against Pakistan in Dacca in November 1969. Burgess scored 2,684 Test runs at an average of 31.20.

His highest one-day score was 47 in the first ever one-day international his country played, against Pakistan in Christchurch in 1973. Burgess retired from first-class cricket after the tour to Australia in 1980/81.

Mark, you were chosen as the New Zealand captain for the series against England, but at the time, Graham Vivian was the captain of your state side Auckland. Was it a surprise to be asked to captain the national side and can you remember how, and when, you were told of the news?

It was a surprise to be asked to become captain of the national side. Not so much for the fact that Graham Vivian was captain of Auckland as he was not really contending for New Zealand at that time. Glenn Turner had been captain in Pakistan and India in 1976, but was not returning to New Zealand as he was organising his benefit year (with Worcestershire) which was occurring during the 1978 summer.

Bevan Congdon was still playing, but did not want to continue as captain and John Parker, who had been vice captain to Turner in Pakistan and India, was not the selectors' preference either for some reason. Frank Cameron eventually persuaded me to agree to do the job. I had never coveted the captaincy, particularly as my cricket availability had become somewhat hit and miss due to the responsibilities of my role at Brittain Wynyard, the firm I had joined in 1972. They had been very generous in allowing me some tours but not others, 1973/74 to Australia and the 1975 World Cup being examples of when I was not available.

On a personal level the captaincy had a very negative effect on my own attitude and performance. I became ridiculously inhibited by the captaincy and so restricted my scoring shots that I handed the initiative to the bowler. If there was one element missing from those times for us, it was the counsel of an experienced coach or manager, who might have given us more confidence in our team and individual performance. We accepted that as individuals we needed to be self-sufficient, and that was fine, but most of us had more ability than we realised and many did not fulfil their potential.

In the press in the UK it was stated, 'Under new captain Mark Burgess they now have a leader positive in outlook and one not afraid of winning.' What captaincy experience had you had, prior to the first Test in Wellington?

I had captained Auckland for a couple of seasons and was fortunate to play under some excellent men with John Sparling,

Graham Vivian and Hedley Howarth captaining sides I played in. I had not, however, and nor had anyone else for that matter, been groomed for the New Zealand job. It generally fell to the most experienced individual and batsman. We certainly suffered still from a slight inferiority complex when playing Australia and England. I think, others may disagree, that we felt we were more likely to get results against India, Pakistan and the West Indies at that point.

Three weeks before the first Test, England (after a pretty disappointing tour of Pakistan where the wickets had been lifeless, cricket disappointing and atmosphere very low-key) played their first tour match against Auckland, at Eden Park, in which you scored an unbeaten 74. Can you remember anything about the game or your innings?

I remember only that we played in good warm conditions on a decent pitch and that I was in good form at that point.

Can you remember how your season in 1977/78 had gone personally in the build-up to the first Test? How much first-class cricket had you played before the match?

In 1978 we were still only playing one round of Plunkett Shield first-class matches, five in total plus a match against a touring team, if there was one. I cannot recall the detail of that season. I must have made enough for the selectors to continue to be interested though.

England had already played several Tests both at home and in Pakistan prior to the first Test at the Basin Reserve. New Zealand's last Test had been almost twelve months earlier against Australia at Eden Park. Did you have any time together, as a team, to prepare for the game?

No, there was no special preparation at all. We assembled three days before the match and went through what was typical for us at the time. Up to three nets for the batsmen and the whole team doing their bit as net bowlers. This included the quicks being Richard Collinge and the two Hadlees. I don't remember there being net bowlers provided.

We had a pre-match dinner the night before the match. Nothing formal and with only the manager, Frank Cameron, who was also chairman of selectors, present. We had no coach, physiotherapist, doctor, et al in those days.

England were the only country, at Test cricket, New Zealand had yet to beat. The English newspapers had thought this absurd especially having produced players of the calibre of Bert Sutcliffe, John Reid and Martin Donnelly. Was there a feeling of expectation amongst the team at the time that you might finally be able to get the monkey off your backs?

We went into the game confident that we were most certainly in with a chance. Mike Brearley was missing and it was Geoffrey Boycott's first Test as captain, and to be fair it was probably not one of England's best ever sides.

All good experienced players, but one thing we did have going for us was the Basin Reserve which in those days was a long way detached from the pleasant atmosphere of Test and county grounds in England.

Shortly after tea on a very windy first day at the Basin Reserve, Bob Willis sent your stumps flying for 9. Can you remember what it was like, not only in that Test, facing Willis?

I have a clear recollection of events. There was close to a gale blowing from the south for most of the match and particularly the first day. Others involved in the match will confirm the presence of a rather odd ridge not far short of a good length when batting at the city end. The ball that bowled me pitched the near side of the ridge and came through at half-stump height between bat and pad. Earlier in the same innings a ball from

Willis rose sharply from the other side of the ridge, and I later discovered that I had cracked a bone.

Facing Bob Willis at any time was a good test. He was always quick and aggressive, and in fact in Christchurch, I copped one from him on the left elbow when he was bowling round the wicket and doing his best to unsettle us. No helmets, arm guards, chest guards in those days.

What was the Basin Reserve, as a ground, like to play on at the time of the Test?

I had a special affection for the Basin and in fact may have better statistics there than anywhere. The Basin Reserve had an entirely different atmosphere in those days. The players' pavilion was side on and seemingly miles away from the action. The pitch ran straight up and down the ground and this meant the breeze, whether from the south or the north, blew directly up and down the ground. It was tough work for the bowlers into it, and great for the quicks with it behind them. Pitch preparation I am certain was a less sophisticated art in those days, but having made that point, the Basin did generally provide pitches that had bounce and pace and were fair to both sides. Every now and then there was a pitch that made it very hard for the batsmen and 1978 was one of those years. The ground changes in the early 80s has produced what I think is now our best Test match venue.

Opener John Wright had played a defiant knock in the New Zealand first innings and reached his fifty in 272 minutes, only two minutes slower than Mudassar Nazar had scored during his record slow-scoring at Lahore the previous December against England! Can you remember anything about Wright's knock?

Everyone who played in the match remembers Wrighty's effort. Bob Willis too will have a clear recollection, including the first-over appeal for a caught behind. As a first-up performance it must rate in importance, as one of, if not the best ever first innings by a Kiwi. He held the first innings together and proved to himself that he truly belonged at that level. At the breaks he seemed concerned that he was too slow, but I and others kept telling him to stick at it and change nothing. As demonstrated by the low scoring, staying in was difficult, as was scoring.

The second day, Saturday, was Bev Congdon's 40th birthday. Can you remember the crowd singing 'Happy Birthday' to Congdon as he went out to resume his innings?

That was a nice moment for Bevan and he played a typically gutsy innings.

New Zealand, after Richard Hadlee had taken 4 for 74, had recorded a first-innings lead of 13. Was there now excitement in the camp of achieving a historic first ever Test win over England?

I wouldn't say that excitement would describe the way we were feeling. We did know, though, that there would be a result, and we needed to do what we could, to have the game go our way.

On the rest day practically all of the team decided to turn up for batting practice. Can you remember that day and also how the pitch was now behaving?

I thought we had all turned up. Maybe Congo (Bevan Congdon) felt he had enough experience to get him by, but the rest of us didn't want to have criticism levelled at us for under-doing things. The pitch had continued to present challenges for the batsmen. The scoring rates off each bowler confirm how difficult things were. Only two batsmen managed half-centuries in the four innings. It was dour stuff all the way.

The fourth day saw just two wickets falling before lunch for 63 runs with I guess most thinking the match might be heading for a draw. Bob Willis stated the progress of the Test had become turgid, with endless maidens, endless blocking and controversial umpiring decisions. Then, no fewer than 17 wickets fell for 101 runs in the next sensational four hours! Bob Willis had taken 5 for 32 and, with England taking some great catches, dismissed you for 123. With England requiring 137, did you then feel your chance of defeating England for the first time had gone?

I think we did. The dressing room was deathly quiet and heads were down. We were all dreadfully disappointed with how our second innings played out. I remember very clearly giving the team a strong telling off about how feeble I thought we had been. It was probably my equivalent of an Alex Ferguson half-time talk when the team had seriously under-performed. Might have been luck, but it might also have had a short-term effect because we were shortly back in the contest.

Then it was the Richard show! Collinge and Hadlee. Mayhem and total panic within the England dressing room! Reporter Dick Brittenden singled out Collinge removing Geoff Boycott for 1 as 'the pivotal moment' to start the collapse. Would you agree?

Dick Brittenden was absolutely on the money. Richard Collinge, inducing Boycott's false stroke, was the turning point. You could sense the immediate change in our attitude. Boycott was the one man capable of grinding out an England victory. Low though the required runs were we knew the difficulties the conditions presented. We certainly sensed that England could fold because all the real difficulties were at the end that Richard Hadlee was bowling at. There was nothing to suggest that the conditions had or would change, and we knew how hard our task had been. We had also witnessed England's struggle in the first innings.

As the wickets fell the atmosphere within the ground must have being incredible. I understand a siren went off every time a wicket fell with a mighty roar, which Brittenden reported 'stifled the vigorous traffic

*noises which always enliven cricket at the Basin Reserve'. Can you
remember the atmosphere on that fourth day and was there a big
crowd inside the ground?*

The atmosphere was electric in the middle. It had its own level
in the crowd which had grown rapidly as we got towards the
end of the day. New Zealand sporting crowds are not known
for creating a real away game tension for visiting teams, but this
was a complete exception. It was as if half of the England boys
didn't particularly fancy it. Hadlee steaming in downwind in a
spell where he gave them little if anything to leave and regular
play and miss balls, lbw appeals, we the slips back about 25 yards
and no one needing to remind the batsmen that they were in a
serious contest. A few batsmen may have been more concerned
with self rather than team survival.

*With England finishing the day on 53 for 8, it would only be a matter
of time, on the final day of the Test, that New Zealand would record
the historic win. Can you remember how you spent the evening before
that final day? I assume you must have been personally quite excited,
knowing that you were going to be the captain that was to have led
New Zealand to that historic win?*

The only thing that could have undone us was the weather. The
boys each went their own way that night, but I know we were all
in bed early and most probably not sleeping too well with what
we had in prospect. The fact that I was captain did not come into
my thinking. All going well we knew we had the goodwill and
support of all those who had gone before us. Men like Donnelly,
Sutcliffe, Reid, Walter Hadlee and all those great servants of the
Kiwi game, would have or were taking great delight in events.
Many of those earlier players had made contact and were right
behind us and we were ready to finalise things for them.

*And so to the final morning. England all out for 64, beaten for the
first time in 48 years by New Zealand in a Test. Was there a big*

crowd in for the final day, and what were your memories when the last wicket fell?

There was a surprisingly large crowd there. I don't even know whether they charged to get in on the final morning.

Geoff Howarth took a neat catch off Richard Hadlee to dismiss Bob Willis and the place erupted. Robert Anderson performed a somewhat strange war dance which would be perfectly acceptable these days. I think Geoff Howarth and I told him to calm down. As stated several times, things were different then.

With the match ending so early in the day, how did the New Zealand team, and also yourself, celebrate? Were there great celebrations and coverage around the country, in the media? E.g. back in your home city of Auckland?

New Zealand Cricket was not all that flush for cash in those days, and we had been checked out of our hotel early, by the-then secretary. We were all ready to go back home by various means. There were a few bottles of champagne opened in the dressing room and then we dispersed. John Parker and I went up to the university tennis courts and had two sets of singles, again in windy conditions.

It was a wonderful moment in New Zealand sport, but none of the players got carried away. Society then didn't take too kindly to individuals who felt they were bigger than the game or the team. Those of us employed outside cricket went back to work for a few days before we reassembled in Christchurch.

Did you have a moment to reflect and pinch yourself that it was you that had been lucky enough to have led the side in that historic Test?

Not really. I think I was lucky to have been in the role and I enjoyed the moment. Geoff Howarth had more of an eye for that sort of thing. He tried unsuccessfully to get me to develop more of a personal profile, and to make something of it personally, but I wasn't raised that way. I think on reflection that I didn't disappoint my parents in sporting matters so I'm happy with that.

Prior to the second Test in Christchurch you, at one point, were doubtful, as you had a broken finger and could not hold a bat. How did you get the injury?

I refer you again to Bob Willis in the Wellington Test. The finger was damaged when Bob hit the side of the ridge on the pitch that was nearest him. The ball rose steeply and smashed into my right forefinger. I was not keen to let the side down by not playing, so I played with the broken finger. It was an injury more common then, than now, and most people just played on.

You recovered, however, to lead the side and were even fielding at second slip on the first day, when you caught both Derek Randall and Graham Roope?

Photos, if available, would show I had two fingers taped together.

The rest day of the Christchurch Test saw both sides being taking out by local farmers? Paul Downton recalled it being 'a spectacular day finished off in style with a barbecue and a "swimming party" at Alan Wright's private home. A day to savour and remember'. Did you socialise much with the England side during their tour to New Zealand?

I remember that day well. Allan Wright was a lovely man as is his nephew John. A young Ian Botham pushed me, casually fully clothed, into the pool. I think we all got on pretty well although I seem to remember Botham making himself a little bit famous, by running out his captain when his team-mates decided the captain was batting too slowly for team needs.

You eventually lost the second Test by 174 runs, after being bowled out for 105 in the second innings. Do you recall much about the Christchurch Test, and how disappointing it was to lose it after Wellington?

It was a big reality check for us and confirmed that we were by no means a world-class side. I was very disappointed that we suffered such a resounding reverse after the excitement of Wellington.

Then to the third Test at your home ground of Eden Park in Auckland. It was a six-day decider! You were attracting some decent crowds to the games, 15,000 on the first day and 24,000 on the second! Was this because of the aftermath of Wellington or were the crowds, in general, very supportive to cricket at that time?

There may have been a few extra in the ground due to Wellington, but cricket was much more strongly supported in the seventies. It had become a competitive series that captured the imagination of Kiwis in general. The mix of players, and the pitch conditions, meant that a six-day draw was not a surprise in the end. It was a flat pitch on which Geoff Howarth and Clive Radley prospered at run rates that would not find favour with our current crop of players.

The New Zealand attitude to Test cricket in the seventies was to firstly try and avoid defeat and secondly play for the win. A drawn series with England, with our player mix, was seen as a very positive outcome. It might have been boring to some, but we took pride in what we had achieved as a team and all thought that a drawn series was a fair outcome.

Did you keep any mementoes from the Basin Reserve Test like a stump? And do you still have your New Zealand Test cap?

I didn't join the race for the stumps and was happy for others to claim them. I still have the cap.

On reflection, in total you played 50 Tests for New Zealand; how would you rate, personally, that win at the Basin Reserve in the first Test amongst the other achievements in your career? And what, for you, were your other career highlights?

In my view the most significant innings I played for New Zealand was the 119 not out, at Dacca, East Pakistan, in 1969. We saved the Test and as a result won the series, a first for New Zealand and in possibly the most difficult country ever to tour and succeed. The Dowling-captained 1969 side was a very good one by the time we reached India and Pakistan.

It must be nice knowing your name is up on the Lord's honours board for your 105 you scored there in 1973?

Of course, and having revisited with family members a few times, it is nice to know the name is up there. Congdon's 1973 team in England was probably the best balanced and most talented side I played in and we did, as referred to earlier, underachieve.

You were raised in Remuera, Auckland, and went on to attend Auckland Grammar School. Do you have fond memories of playing sport at school?

I was very fortunate to begin my sporting career at Remuera Primary School, where there were teachers interested in developing young people with both an academic and a sporting emphasis.

We found the same at Remuera Intermediate, and it was there that I was able to play football for the first time, under a teacher who played in the local Northern Premier League. We were encouraged to treat the game and the opposition with respect. We now live overlooking Remuera Intermediate where our children were and now a grandson is a pupil.

You actually made your first-class debut, aged 19, for a New Zealand Under-23 XI before actually playing for Auckland. Do you remember anything about this game?

My first-class debut was not particularly noteworthy. I didn't get off the mark in the first innings and didn't reach double figures in the second. Not surprisingly the Auckland selectors took a few more years to show any interest in me. I was at that time much more focused on football, and had played for the full Auckland team from the age of 17, and in the lower sixth form at Auckland Grammar. I hadn't had too much ambition cricket-wise and was chosen for the New Zealand Under-23 team after a Rothmans Tournament. I must have had a reasonable return.

It must have been a very proud moment for both your family and yourself when you made your debut for Auckland?

My parents were delighted of course and fully supportive of the selectors' decision. My cricket progress had possibly been impeded a little by the fact that, in those days, the club system in Auckland meant you could only play for the club in whose area you lived. Eastern, the club I was entitled to play for, was made up of five current or ex-New Zealand representatives, four Auckland players, and a couple of others. Opportunities for me to display my talents were limited. Geoff Rabone, the captain, was an off-spinner so that didn't help and I batted at nine on the rare occasions we lost enough wickets. I applied for a transfer to Grafton, on the grounds explained, and there followed several weeks of great ill feeling and press coverage of the drama. Good sense prevailed fortunately, and I was allowed to make the move, and the following season they dispensed with the district scheme.

Your maiden first-class century was actually made in India in 1968, whilst playing some matches to raise money for the Koyna Relief

Fund. I understand you played with several other international players. Can you remember much about the games and tour?

It was a great experience for a young man, and followed a decent time I had in the four-Test series against India, led by the Nawab of Pataudi. We played one match at the Brabourne Stadium, in Bombay, where each of the four days was played in front of fully sold-out crowds. The second match was played on matting and was a first-class fixture. Graham Dowling and I were driven from Bombay to Goa by Polly Umrigar, a former Indian great who was a heavy scorer against New Zealand touring teams.

Amongst the international players we had Fred Trueman, Raman Subba Row, Brian Statham, Norman O'Neill and John Wardle. Conditions were unlike any I had experienced. It was very hot and humid with very noisy energetic crowds who knew the game. Meeting and playing with that group was very broadening for me. They were amusing company and still players proud of what they had done in the game and keen to show their best.

(Note: The Koynanagar earthquake had occurred near Koynanagar town in Maharashtra, India, on 11 December 1967, and had claimed at least 180 lives and injured over 1,500, with over 80% of the houses damaged in the Koynanagar township.)

You were New Zealand Footballer of the Year in 1965. Tell us about your football career, Mark.

I absolutely loved football and had been brought up with a family affiliation with West Ham. I played junior football at the Eden Club, and managed to get myself into age group teams along the way, and to then fit the eye of all of the immigrant coaches looking after U18, U21 and U23 teams. I was very lucky to play for some football coaches who not only knew the game very well, but gave me a confidence I never really felt with my cricket.

Things are different now as we export all our better players, but in my time New Zealand was an attractive place to emigrate to, as a place to find solid employment. Across a very broad mix of trades, football clubs assisted players who were, or had, played at a good level in the UK and who would add to clubs' experience at National League and lower league competition level.

What position did you play ?

I was a midfielder and particularly liked playing for the coaches who encouraged possession, and pass and move. You never lose your love of the game and I still like to think your touch never leaves you.

In 1967 you played for New Zealand in an unofficial match against Manchester United. Can you recall which players you played against in that game and what the experience was like?

Manchester United were more than useful. We played them twice and they hammered us both times. Juan Schwanner our coach insisted on us trying to play, rather than setting up to defend, and keep the score down. They had Stepney, Kidd, Crerand, Foulkes, Aston, Dunne, Cantwell, Sadler, Stiles, Law, Charlton, Best and their record in the next few years was testament to their quality. Again I was fortunate to be part of what was a moment in New Zealand sport that people remember.

It sounds like you have a big passion for football, serving for over thirty years on the New Zealand Soccer Council. Do you follow the game in the UK and do you have a favourite team?

It was actually a much shorter spell in the NZFA. Six years. I very much enjoyed the experience, but became involved on the Oceania Football Confederation as the New Zealand delegate, and in the end I resigned to get away from the politics of OFC and FIFA. Much has emerged in recent weeks that explain the reasons I left. I found myself hitting my head against a brick wall.

The New Zealand soccer team has participated in two World Cup finals in Spain in 1982 and South Africa in 2010. You must have been very proud of New Zealand's achievements going unbeaten in 2010 and even drawing 1-1 against Italy?

The boys did a great job and being the only unbeaten team was incredible. We were very proud of course and they were recognised, being named the 'Team of the Year'. No mean feat when up against the All Blacks and the netballers and rowers who are outstanding always.

Appendix D:

Interview with Mudassar Nazar

PAKISTAN right-hand opening batsman Mudassar Nazar played 76 Tests and 122 one-day internationals between 1976 and 1989. During England's tour to Pakistan in 1977, Mudassar broke the record for scoring the slowest Test century, a record that still stands to this day. Mudassar now coaches for the ICC Cricket Academy, and whilst on tour with an Academy team to the UK in July 2015, I got in touch with him whilst he was in Taunton to ask him about not only that innings, but his career in general as well.

Mudassar Nazar, son of Pakistan Test cricketer Nazar Mohammad, made his Test debut against Australia in Adelaide in 1976 with his last being against New Zealand in Auckland in February 1989. After playing league cricket in both Pakistan and England, Mudassar had two stints as coach to Pakistan in 1993 and 2001 as well as with Kenya in 2005.

Mudassar, you had a distinguished Test career for Pakistan, playing 76 Tests, scoring over 4,000 runs and averaging 38.09. You made your Test debut against Australia in Adelaide, in December 1976. What was it like opening the batting and facing the might of Dennis Lillee and Jeff Thomson? Who both, it must be said, failed to get you out in both innings!

Prior to the Test match at Adelaide we had been in Australia for a long time. In those times if you were not a regular player in the team you did not get many opportunities to practice as the senior players took up all the time available.

Sadiq got injured on the eve of the game and now they looked for an opening partner for Majid. Up till now I had not batted once in the nets and neither had I played any games. Mushtaq gave Salim Altaf a new ball and told him to take me to the nets. It had started to get dark. He bowled three balls at me and said he has had enough. This was my total preparation to face Lillee and Thomson. On the match day Lillee bowled the first over and it looked as though he was bowling a tennis ball because the ball was bouncing so much. Thomson bowled the first ball to me and all of his fielders were behind me. There were only fine leg and cover point that were not in a catching position. Both bowled blisteringly fast, but I survived for over an hour.

Gilmour got me out when suddenly I relaxed after Lillee was taken off. In the second innings Majid and I put on over 60 runs. Lillee was bowling four bouncers an over. Halfway through I said to Majid I was going to hook him. Instead of telling me to steady on he said what are you waiting for? I went for a hook and got hit on the back of my head. Everyone thought I was dead. Luckily I jumped up and carried on batting. Kerry O'Keefe had me caught behind on 26. We bowled and fielded brilliantly on the last day to save the game. Asif and Zaheer batted really well for us.

(This drawn Test was the first of a three-match series which ended 1-1, with Pakistan winning the third and final Test in Sydney.)

England toured Pakistan in 1977, and you first came up against them in a low-scoring drawn match playing for the BCCP Patron's XI, at the Pindi Club Ground in Rawalpindi. Can you remember anything about the game in which you scored 9 and 11?

I remember the match at Rawalpindi was played on a wet pitch and it took a lot of spin. Although England took wickets with their spinners we put them under pressure with our seam bowlers. My standout memory is me taking an outstanding left-handed catch to dismiss Derek Randall at second slip.

Your second Test appearance for Pakistan was at the Gaddafi Stadium in Lahore, the city where you were born, in the first Test against England in December 1977. It must have been a proud moment for you, playing your first home Test, in your home city?

I always wanted to play a Test match at Lahore. It was my home ground and luckily I was able to score three Test centuries there.

Can you remember any instructions from your captain Wasim Bari on how you should approach your innings that day?

Prior to this series, we had most of our senior players banned for their role in the Packer affair. The Pakistan Cricket Board did not want us to lose the match and the series. They wanted to keep these seniors out of the game forever. We were under instruction to make sure we did not lose the game.

Batting first in the Test after winning the toss, the first day saw Pakistan finish the day on 164 for 2 off 63 overs. You closed on 52 not out. Playing a patient innings that day you reached 50 after 170 minutes and ended the 300-minute day on 52!

At tea on the first day I was on 48 and hit Bob Willis for four through the covers. At that juncture I wanted to score at a better rate. A couple of overs later I came out of the crease to hit Miller and was lucky not to get out.

After the over, our manager Imtiaz sent me a message to buckle down and play for the tea interval. I immediately put the block on, but did not realise for a long time I was still on 52. Next day Miandad batted a long time with me. We always ran well together and if it was not for Miandad's running between the wickets I would still be batting on 52.

Mudassar, you reached 99 twenty-five minutes before tea on the second day with some spectators believing you had reached your hundred, invading the pitch to congratulate you. This resulted in the police coming on to the pitch to chase them off, which ended up causing a riot!

I remember being extremely anxious while waiting for the riot to finish. I kept panicking if the game might be called off and I would remain on 99.

Things settled down after the umpires had wisely decided to take an early tea. It must have been a very proud moment for you to have reached your debut Test century? Then spinner Geoff Miller got you out, caught and bowled. Can you remember the dismissal?

Luckily we resumed and Miandad called for a quick single and I was able to complete my century. Lots of people poured on to the field to congratulate me. Some of them gave me money too. One such guy told me he enjoyed my hundred, but if I did not start to hit out then he would come back and beat me up. I took his advice and promptly hit Miller for three consecutive fours. Going for the fourth boundary I was caught and bowled.

It had taken you nine hours and seventeen minutes to reach your hundred, breaking the record for the slowest century in Test cricket by twelve minutes, which still stands today. Looking back now, you must be very proud of this record? Even if at the time it came in for a lot of criticism because it was so slow. But you did your job for your country and it is an amazing achievement.

I have always had mixed feelings for this record. One thing is sure, that this record will always belong to me. Only Boycott would have beaten it. In fact had he scored a century in the same game he would have beaten it. He scored 65 and it had taken him longer than my 65. I had the utmost respect for him. He was such a great player. He was the first one to come forward and congratulate me.

And then to the third day's play and more rioting, which put the whole England tour into jeopardy. The rioting caused mainly by the appearance of Nusrat Bhutto, which even resulted in a fire being started in the Women's Enclosure!

The Test was marred again when Nusrat Bhutto decided to come to the game and use the crowd for disruption to make a point against the ruling regime. It was very unfortunate, but politicians in Pakistan always use cricket to advance their needs.

The Test series eventually ended in a 0-0 draw. You scored 66 in the second Test in Hyderabad and 76 in Karachi in the third. Can you remember much about those Tests?

The next two Test matches were drawn as well. I was in great form and felt I should have scored another hundred in Karachi. On 76 I pulled a rank bad ball from Edmonds only to mishit it to mid-on.

Did you admire the batting of England opener Geoffrey Boycott?

For me it was an eye-opener to watch Boycott bat against our spinners. He batted just like the Asian batsmen. Always in the correct position to hit the ball with the spin.

The tour by England took place in the shadow of Kerry Packer's World Series Cricket. What were your thoughts on Packer at the time and also looking back now?

I have always admired Kerry Packer and what he has done for cricket. I agreed to sign for him, but he, in the meantime, got the rights he was looking for and I, along with many other Pakistani players, missed out. I also did not like the attitude of the authorities to ban players. Players were right in trying to earn a decent living.

You played in total 76 Tests for Pakistan between 1976 and 1989. A long-distinguished Test career. Which innings would you say was the best you played?

I thought my best innings was when I scored a century and carried my bat through in Lahore against India. It was on a very wet pitch and Kapil was making our life very difficult. Gavaskar dropped me in the slips very early on.

(The innings Mudassar mentions was the fifth Test against India in Lahore in January 1983.)

On 23 December 1977 you made your one-day debut for Pakistan against England in Sialkot, becoming the 21st player to represent your country. Can you remember much about your debut?

I played a lot of one-day cricket. but I do not remember much about my debut game.

You successfully went on to make 122 one-day appearances for your country. What would you say was your best ODI innings?

My best knock was against Australia in Sharjah where I scored 95. We needed four to win and I went for a six only to be bowled by Bruce Reid.

(The match was on 11 April 1986 in the Ausral-Asia Cup in which Pakistan won by eight wickets. Mudassar put on 115 for the second wicket with Rameez Raja.)

You played League Cricket in the north of England?

I spent nine years with Burnley, three with Horwich, eight years with Bolton and a few more with different clubs in Lancashire.

And then you played Minor Counties cricket for Cheshire between 1980 and 1985. Were you ever approached, or would have liked, to have played first-class county cricket?

There was only one county, Surrey, who showed some interest, but then they signed Sylvester Clarke which proved a great signing for them. In 1976 I wrote to a few counties and they were prepared to give me a few second XI games, but I refused. Looking back I should have taken that route and it might have proved a route map for me.

In 1985 Western Australia were keen to sign me, but their season conflicted with my Test engagements and I wanted to pursue more Test cricket. So I let it go. I absolutely loved playing for Cheshire though.

Your father Nazar Mohammad was also an opening batsman for Pakistan. He became the first Pakistan batsman to carry his bat through an innings against India in Lucknow in October 1952. Then you became the second Pakistani to achieve the feat thirty-one years later!

While I always have had mixed feelings about my slowest hundred, but 'father and son', who carried their bat through the innings, makes me very proud. My father was always very proud of it as well.

Appendix E:

Where Are They Now?

The England Tour Party 1977/78

Mike Brearley (Middlesex)
Brearley played 39 Tests for England (31 as captain), averaging 22.89 in 66 Test innings. He went on to become president of the MCC in 2007/08 and pursued a career as a writer (his book *The Art of Captaincy* was published in 1985) and psychoanalyst, serving as president of the British Psychoanalytical Society between 2008 and 2010.

Geoff Boycott (Yorkshire)
Boycott played his last Test for England, his 108th, against India in 1982. He averaged 47.72 for his country. His first-class career saw him hit 151 first-class centuries. After his playing career ended, Boycott became an outspoken and controversial commentator on both radio and television, including BBC's *Test Match Special*. He was president of Yorkshire between March 2012 and March 2014.

Ian Botham (Somerset)
Botham is generally regarded as England's greatest all-rounder. His England career lasted from 1976 until 1992 in which he played 102 Tests and 116 ODIs. He scored 14 centuries and

took 383 wickets in Test cricket. He was also England's leading Test wicket-taker until April 2015 when he was surpassed by James Anderson. He holds numerous records in Test cricket and the Ashes of 1981 will always be remembered as 'Botham's Ashes'. Botham has been a prodigious fundraiser for charity and was awarded a knighthood in recognition of this. Botham is currently a commentator on Sky Television.

Geoff Cope (Yorkshire)

Spinner Cope played only three Test matches for England (all in Pakistan in 1977) and played first-class cricket for Yorkshire between 1966 and 1980. After cricket, Cope was elected on to the Yorkshire committee and was appointed director of cricket in 2002. Cope is now officially registered blind, but though his peripheral vision is very poor, he can still see directly in front of him.

Paul Downton (Kent)

Between 1977 and 1989 wicket-keeper Downton played 30 Tests and 28 ODIs for England and went on to finish his county career with Middlesex. His career ended when he suffered a freak eye injury, in which a bail lodged in his eye when he was standing up to the stumps. He subsequently became a stockbroker in the City. Downton was appointed managing director of the England and Wales Cricket Board from 1 February 2014, but was dismissed from the post on 8 April 2015.

Phil Edmonds (Middlesex)

Edmonds went on to play 51 Tests (taking 125 wickets) and 29 ODIs for England before retiring in 1992. Edmonds at times could be not only charming, but controversial as well. When England were playing a Test in Calcutta on their 1984/85 tour, and with India's batsmen playing at a snail's pace towards a draw, Edmonds produced a copy of *The Daily Telegraph* and proceeded to read it whilst fielding at square leg! After cricket, Edmonds was chairman of several companies including the

Central African Mining & Exploration Company. In July 2012 it was reported he had an estimated fortune of £14 million.

Mike Gatting (Middlesex)

Gatting, who made his Test debut on the tour to Pakistan, went on to play 79 Tests and 92 ODIs for England in which he scored ten Test centuries. He captained England in 23 Tests including an Ashes series victory in Australia in 1986/87. He was sacked as England captain after an alleged encounter with a barmaid. Gatting toured South Africa as captain of the rebel tour party in 1990 and became president of the MCC in 2013 during the bicentenary of Lord's.

Mike Hendrick (Derbyshire)

Right-arm fast-medium bowler Hendrick played 30 Tests and 22 ODIs for England between 1973 and 1981. His 770 first-class wickets came at an impressive cost of just 20 apiece. His career saw him go on the first rebel tour to South Africa, which incurred a three-year ban from Test cricket. After retiring, Hendrick became popular on the after-dinner speech circuit and in 1992 became the coach at Nottinghamshire. In-between 1995 and 2000 he was bowling coach for Ireland and then between 2004 and 2008 for Derbyshire before returning to Nottinghamshire. Early 2015 saw Hendrick help out as the bowling coach with the Minor Counties side, Shropshire.

John Lever (Essex)

Left-arm fast-medium bowler Lever played in 21 Tests and 22 ODIs for England from 1976 to 1986. Lever played for Essex for 22 years and was awarded an MBE for his services to cricket. He went on the 1982 rebel tour to South Africa and spent many winters there playing for Natal. In 1986 Lever earned another, rather belated, Test cap at the age of 37. Lever went on to teach PE at Bancroft's School and become bowling coach at Middlesex.

Geoff Miller (Derbyshire)

Miller's career lasted from 1973 to 1989 in which he played 34 Tests and 25 ODIs for England. Miller, a correct right-handed batsman and reliable right-arm off-break bowler, never scored a century for England despite coming close twice, scoring 98 against Pakistan away in 1977/78 and India at home in 1982. In January 2008 he was elected National Selector and remained in the post until he retired in 2013. He had served on the panel of selectors since 2000. Miller was also a popular after-dinner speaker and was awarded the OBE in 2014.

Chris Old (Yorkshire)

Old played 46 Tests for England between 1972 and 1981, taking 143 wickets, as well as appearing in 32 ODIs. He became Yorkshire captain in 1981, but it was not a happy period and the next season he relinquished the position. After finishing his first-class career with three seasons with Warwickshire in 1985, Old turned out in the Minor Counties for Northumberland for eight matches in 1987. Old would surely have played more Test cricket, but was prone to injuries. Old eventually owned a fish and chip restaurant in Praa Sands, Cornwall, between 2002 and 2009, but amid the economic recession he sold it. It was last reported in 2012 that he was working in the supermarket Sainsbury's and still coaches a local cricket club in Falmouth.

Derek Randall (Nottinghamshire)

The fondly admired Randall played 47 Tests and 49 ODIs for England. He was an excellent cover fielder and often a selectorial scapegoat for England's failings. After retiring in 1993 he later turned out for Suffolk in the Minor Counties playing, aged 49, for them in the NatWest Trophy. He coached at Cambridge University and Bedford School when Alistair Cook came through the school's first XI, with Randall recommending Cook be picked for the ECB National Academy. He also coached Bedfordshire and wrote *The Young Player's Guide to Cricket*.

Graham Roope (Surrey)

Roope went on to play 21 Tests and eight ODIs for England between 1973 and 1978. Surrey batsman Roope scored 19,116 runs in 403 first-class matches. Tall and wiry in stature, Roope was an excellent slip fielder and after retiring played for Farsley Cricket Club. He coached at Ampleforth College and Woodhouse Grove School (where he was also head groundsman). In 2006, aged 60, Roope died suddenly of a heart attack whilst on a charity cricket tour in St George's, Grenada.

Brian Rose (Somerset)

Somerset batsman Rose played nine Tests and two ODIs for England and scored over 13,000 first-class runs in a career between 1969 and 1987. Rose led Somerset to their first ever trophies, the Gillette Cup and the John Player League, in 1979. He went on to become both chairman and director of cricket at Taunton.

Bob Taylor (Derbyshire)

Taylor kept wicket for England in 57 Tests and 27 ODIs between 1971 and 1984. He took 167 catches and made seven stumpings in Test cricket. His 1,649 dismissals (1,473 caught and 176 stumped) in 639 games remains a first-class record. During the 1986 New Zealand Test at Lord's, Taylor was present in a hospitality tent when Bruce French got injured. After trialing Bill Athey behind the wicket, Jeremy Coney, the New Zealand captain, permitted Taylor to play for the remainder of the day, during which he kept wicket without a blemish. Taylor suffered a heart attack at the beginning of July 2015 and underwent a heart by-pass operation.

Bob Willis (Warwickshire)

Willis ended with 325 Test wickets in 1984 at 25.20 runs per wicket and is currently England's third highest wicket-taker behind Ian Botham and James Anderson. Willis took a Test career best 8 for 43 at Headingley in the 1981 Ashes Test (one of the all-time great Test bowling performances). Willis captained the England team in 18 Tests and 28 ODI matches between June 1982 and March 1984. Willis now works as a cricket commentator and expert on Sky Sports.

Ken Barrington (**Manager**)

Manager Ken Barrington had played 82 Tests for England between 1955 and 1968 and had played for one county throughout his career, Surrey. He was an England selector between 1975 and 1981 and was a regular tour manager. Barrington sadly died, aged just 50, from a second heart attack at Needham's Point in Barbados on 14 March 1981 during the third Test at Bridgetown, where he had made his maiden Test century 21 years before. Seven hundred mourners turned out for Barrington's memorial service at Southwark Cathedral where the service was led by ex-England captain David Sheppard and saw actor and comedian Harry Secombe sing 'Amazing Grace'.

Appendix F:

Tour memorabilia

MCC Tour Pakistan and New Zealand 1977-78 Players & Officials Tour Itinerary Booklet printed by the MCC Printing Press (A 20-page A6-size itinerary which included a list of matches, travel arrangements, hotels, postal arrangements, etc)

Official Autograph Sheet signed by all of the 19 England Touring Party at the start of the tour.

In Pakistan

Official Tour Photo Print signed round the border by all 19 of the Touring Squad. Printed by Allied Photo Co, Lahore

Official Christmas Card. Signed inside by manager Ken Barrington and all of the Playing Squad

Issued Programmes for Matches unless stated:-

BCCP Patron's XI v England, Rawalpindi

United Bank XI v England, Faisalabad

North West Frontier XI v England, Peshawar (not known)

Pakistan v England 1st Test, Lahore

Pakistan v England 1st ODI, Sahiwal (not known)

Habib Bank XI v England, Lahore

Pakistan v England 2nd ODI, Sialkot

Pakistan v England 2nd Test, Hyderabad

Punjab XI v England, Bahawalpur (not known)

Pakistan v England 3rd ODI, Lahore (not known)

Sind XI v England, Karachi

Pakistan v England 3rd Test, Karachi

In New Zealand

Official 'Rothmans' Autograph Sheet signed by all of the 19 England Touring Party for the New Zealand leg of the tour

Four-page folded card menu for a dinner given by the New Zealand Cricket Council in honour of the England team

Issued Programmes:-

Auckland v England, Auckland

Northern Districts v England, Hamilton

Central Districts v England, New Plymouth

Canterbury v England, Christchurch

New Zealand v England 1st Test, Wellington

Otago v England, Dunedin

Young New Zealand v England, Temuka ***

New Zealand v England 2nd Test, Christchurch

New Zealand v England 3rd Test, Auckland

Rothmans Programmes were issued for all nine tour matches except
* *against Young New Zealand when a large four-page scorecard was issued.*

The Official England Scorebook from the tour is held in the MCC Archives at Lord's. Archive Reference: MCC/CRI/4/1/30

Bibliography

Books

In my research for *In The Shadow Of Packer,* I have consulted these books below, but most of them it must be added, only briefly.

Pakistan Book of Cricket 1978-79. Edited by Qamar Ahmed (1979)

The 1978 Shell Cricket Almanack of New Zealand. Edited by A.H. Carman. 30th year (1979)

1979 *Wisden Cricketers' Almanack* (Macdonald and Janes)

The Art of Captaincy – Mike Brearley (Channel 4 / Pan MacMillan)

Lasting the Pace – Bob Willis (Collins)

The Cricket Revolution – Bob Willis with Pat Murphy (Book Club Associates)

Leading From The Front – Mike Gatting (Queen Anne Press)

Geoff Boycott – *The Autobiography* (Pan MacMillan)

Ian Botham – *Head On* (Ebury Press)

Ian Botham – *Don't Tell Kath* (Harper Collins Willow)

Derek Randall – *The Sun Has Got His Hat On* (Collins)

Derek Randall – *Rags* (Sport In Print)

Phil Edmonds – A Singular Man by Simon Barnes (Kingswood)

Bob Taylor – *Standing Up Standing Back* (Willow Books)

R.T. Brittenden – *England Skittled* (Nag's Head Press)

Gideon Haigh – *The Cricket War 'The Inside Story of Kerry Packer's World Series Cricket'* (Melbourne University Press)

Newspapers and Magazines
The Cricketer International, The Daily Telegraph, Sunday Telegraph, The Daily Mail, The Daily Express, The Guardian, The Observer, The Sunday Express, The Times, Sportstimes, The 1978 New Zealand Tour of England Official Brochure, The New Zealand Herald, The Dominion Post, The Christchurch Press and *The Otago Daily Times.*